More Praise for *Finding the Deep River Within*

"This practical guide is full of tools and encouragement to help overworked, overcommitted women regain balance and spiritual contentment and would be a great project to tackle with a reading group or buddy.… A comforting and stimulating how-to, *Finding the Deep River Within* has powerful inner and outer implications."
—*Body+Soul*

"If you can wait at a red light without applying makeup or practicing Italian verbs with a CD, this book is not for you. For the rest of us, Seixas has a message: Slow down!"
—*Brandeis University Magazine*

"When things get crazy, and I need to let go, I often use the image of floating on my back, trusting the river, allowing it to take me where it will. Now I have a book to read while floating! Abby Seixas's beautifully written *Finding the Deep River Within* is a wise and fluid book—as clear as a mountain stream and as deep as the ocean."
—Elizabeth Lesser, cofounder, Omega Institute, and author, *Broken Open: How Difficult Times Can Help Us Grow*

"Abby Seixas's work is a blessing. As a psychotherapist, teacher, speaker, and author, I know how much people need to hear what she has to say. *Finding the Deep River Within* belongs on the bookshelves of every therapist who works with women—not only to give to clients, but for their own self-care. I am already recommending it to clients and friends."
—Dr. Dorothy Firman, coauthor, *Daughters and Mothers, Making It Work; Chicken Soup for the Mother and Daughter Soul*, and the forthcoming *Chicken Soup for the Mother and Daughter Soul 2*

"This book is terrific. It reads like a letter from your best friend. It's smart and helpful without being pedantic. Seixas's stories inspire, and her six practices give down-to-earth tools for bringing

balance and joy into your daily life. You'll want to share *Finding the Deep River Within* with your sister, your mother, daughter, aunt, office mate, women friends… all the women in your life, and then, make sure you leave it around for the guys to read it too."
—Bob Kriegel, Ph.D., and Marilyn Harris Kriegel, MS, coauthors, *The C-Zone: Peak Performance Under Pressure*

"*Finding the Deep River Within* is one of those rare books in which you recognize yourself and what you need from the very first page. Blending wisdom with compassion, inspiration with practical tools, Seixas meets us where we are and gently guides us toward wholeness."
—Rachael Freed, author, *Women's Lives, Women's Legacies: Passing Your Beliefs and Blessings to Future Generations* and *The Women's Legacies Workbook for the Busy Woman*

"Everyone whose life is too busy and is seeking a deeper source of nourishment should read this book. Both beginners and experienced students of the inner life will savor its timeless and timely wisdom and find practical tools for transforming their lives from the inside out."
—Jeffrey Rossman, Ph.D., director, Behavioral Health, Canyon Ranch, Lenox, Massachusetts

Finding the Deep River Within

A Woman's Guide to Recovering Balance and Meaning in Everyday Life

Abby Seixas

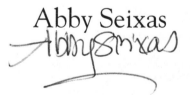

JOSSEY-BASS
A Wiley Imprint
www.josseybass.com

Published by Jossey-Bass
A Wiley Imprint
989 Market Street, San Francisco, CA 94103-1741   www.josseybass.com

Jossey-Bass books and products are available through most bookstores. To contact Jossey-Bass directly call our Customer Care Department within the U.S. at 800-956-7739, outside the U.S. at 317-572-3986, or fax 317-572-4002.

Jossey-Bass also publishes its books in a variety of electronic formats. Some content that appears in print may not be available in electronic books.

Library of Congress Cataloging-in-Publication Data

Seixas, Abby, date.
   Finding the deep river within: a woman's guide to recovering balance and meaning in everyday life / Abby Seixas.
        p. cm.
   Includes bibliographical references and index.
   ISBN-13: 978-0-7879-8097–9 (cloth: alk. paper)
   ISBN-10: 0-7879-8097-8 (cloth: alk. paper)
   ISBN-13: 978-0-7879-9749-6 (paperback)
   ISBN-10: 0-7879-9749-8 (paperback)
   1. Women—Conduct of life. 2. Women—Psychology. I. Title.
BJ1610.S42 2006
158.1082—dc22   2006014414

Printed in the United States of America
FIRST EDITION
HB Printing   10 9 8 7 6 5 4 3 2
PB Printing   10 9 8 7 6 5 4 3 2 1

Contents

Deep River Exercises and Practices

The Six Deep River Practices

For Rachel and Eli,
for their generation, and for those that follow.
May the river flow on.

Acknowledgments

Writing this book has been as much an experience of gratitude and grace as of patience and perseverance. The hard part was sitting down at the computer day after day after day. The remarkable gift has been the kind-spirited support of so many generous and wonderful people.

I first want to thank all the women—clients and group members—who entrusted me with their stories. Your struggles and victories were a large part of the inspiration to write this book. In drawing from your experiences, I have changed names and other identifying information and, in some cases, created composite examples to illustrate a point. But the flesh on the bones of this book's ideas comes from you. I am grateful for your willingness to share so much of yourselves with me and for your enthusiasm and encouragement to *get the book written!*

Several years ago, I had a conversation with Bill Joiner that, unbeknownst to me at the time, was the moment of conception for this book. I am grateful for the mysterious workings of Spirit that led us to help each other put our ideas to paper, and to you, Bill, for your support along the way.

Thanks to Halé and Steven Schatz, who, along with Bill, led me to my agent, Sabine Hrechdakian. Halé, thank you also for writing a book before me! . . . and for your generosity in passing along what you learned.

Thank you Sabine, agent extraordinaire, for seeing, right from the start, how this book could help women. I am grateful for your steady enthusiasm, sound advice, and patient explanations of how the publishing world works. I understand that it's not a given to have such support from an agent, and I consider myself lucky.

I am also indebted to the staff at Jossey-Bass, including my wonderful editor, Sheryl Fullerton. Sheryl, you have been not just an editor but a teacher, making me a better writer despite myself. Your wise guidance, delivered with a soft touch, was just the right combination to keep me going. The result is a grateful author and a better book. Thank you for your wisdom, your patience, and your talent as a wordsmith.

My ability to write a book about the sustaining force of the Deep River within was only possible because of the *other* sustaining force in my life: my circle of friends, family, and colleagues. There are many in this circle whose encouragement I am deeply grateful for. Thanks to all of you—too many to name here—for the gift of your presence in my life; among these, I am indebted to the following people not only for their overall support of this project but for help in specific ways: Jean Guenther, for your input about befriending feelings and for your cards, phone calls, and other forms of cheerleading, with and without bullhorn; John Firman and Ann Gila, for looking at parts of the manuscript at the start, endorsing it early on, and helping with psychosynthesis-related questions; Toni Brooks, for helping me track down outside readers; Kate Wylie, for your input on presence in Chapter Eight; Anne Yeomans, for help with the section on our role as women in Chapter Ten; Rachel Naomi Remen, for looking at the manuscript, giving it your blessing, and supporting this book's birth through your recommendation; Jeff Rossman, for referring women to my groups and endorsing my work and the book early on; Marilyn and Bob Kriegel, for great advice on how to spread the word, and encouragement to do so; and Didi Firman, my deep gratitude for your unequivocal support for this project from the beginning, for taking time to read the manuscript at the end, and for your wise and helpful feedback.

I am also indebted to Dana Standish for pinch-editing in the midst of far more important crises and doing a fabulous job; to Susan Callaghan for jumping on board with total willingness to help redesign the Deep River diagram; to Jenifer Lippincott for sharing tips on proposal writing and going to bat for me when I was seeking an agent; to Julie Cancio for rescuing me in my darkest permissions-seeking hour; and to Pat Reinstein for input on Chapter Six and for all the work that came before. Although I didn't know it then, it was all preparation for being able to do this. I am also deeply grateful to Emily Hutcheson, who walked with me, literally and figuratively, through each step of writing this book. Thank you for being a tirelessly willing sounding board, for reading the manuscript, and for your abiding friendship.

Thank you to my brothers Peter and Noah Seixas for asking, "How's the book going?" and actually being willing to listen to the answer; to my mother, Judith Seixas, for your patience while I got through this project—I'm proud to follow in your footsteps as a first-time author in her fifties; and to my late father, Frank Seixas, who would have supported me in this as he supported me in every endeavor I undertook while he was alive. And thank you to Rachel and Eli Horowitz—for the joy you give me and for providing an empty nest just in time.

There are two people I want to acknowledge in the without-whom-it-couldn't-have-been-done category. The first is Sara Hunter, my book angel. I went for tea at Sara's one day and somehow left ready to write a book. My deepest gratitude to you, Sara, for being the conduit for the mysterious spark that ignited the writing of this book; for shepherding me through the proposal stage; for advising, editing, and sharing all your skill and savvy about writing and publishing; for doing a final pass on the manuscript; and for cheering me on always with your infectious optimism. At first, I marveled at how you gave your time and attention so freely and fully. Now I see that this is just how you live your life. I am blessed to have been in the right place at the right time for the sunshine of your warmhearted attention to fall on me.

Finally, I give thanks to—and for—my husband and life partner, Mark Horowitz. Your loving support—your wholehearted "yes" to this project, to the idea for the Deep River groups originally, and to just about anything that has furthered my growth, personally and professionally—is a lifelong gift beyond measure. Thank you for your willingness to be my first reader and editor of every single word, to bring your intelligent mind and good sense to bear wherever they were needed, to gently prod me and put up with my resistance when something needed fixing, to brainstorm ideas and talk me through stuck places at all hours of the day or night, to take on my computer crises as if they were your own (also at all hours of the day or night), to help me get out of my own way, to make me laugh, to celebrate my victories and empathize with my struggles. I don't know how I got to be so fortunate as to have my own live-in mensch. And just for the record, *you* told me, a long time before anyone else, and before I was ready, that I had a book to write.

Introduction

I slept well until I had children. Like many mothers, by the time I had put in six or eight years of interrupted or could-easily-be-interrupted sleep, the habit of waking at night was deeply engrained. Over the years, in my 3 A.M. sessions, I've tried any number of ways of dealing with being awake when I don't want to be, from counting backward as I breathe deeply to taking prescription sleep medication. Often during these wakeful times, my mind spins anxiously forward to everything I have to do in the coming day, how *much* is on The List, how *tired* I might feel if I can't get back to sleep, which will mean getting even further behind as I drag myself through the day . . . and so on. For obvious reasons, this train of thought doesn't soothe me back into a deep and restful sleep.

But occasionally, I have a very different experience in the middle of the night. I get out of bed. I go downstairs, wrap a blanket around me, and sit on the living room couch. Sometimes I light a candle, and sometimes I sit in the dark. Sometimes I meditate, but mostly I just sit there. As I surrender to being awake, heavy eyelids and all, something shifts inside me. I find I am no longer fighting myself, fighting the night. I relax and begin to notice how quiet it is. In the stillness, my body softens and I breathe more deeply. I feel as though I'm dropping down into myself, as if I am greeting an old, dear, trusted friend. Sometimes I think about my life, but more often I just feel gratitude for *having* a life, for being alive. Or I just sit there in an experience not easy to articulate. It feels as if I am finding myself again, coming home to myself. This sense of fullness or wholeness makes not-enough-sleep seem a much smaller issue than it was an hour before. Often, I return to bed. Whether or not I go back to sleep, I am deeply renewed.

When I drop down into myself in those quiet hours of the night, it feels as though I have tapped into a deep river that runs strongly beneath the busyness of my daily life. When I allow myself to fully experience this deep river within, I connect not only with myself and what matters most to me but also with a powerful stream of silence, mystery, clarity, aliveness. . . . I seem to tap into a universal source, available to us all, of deeply nourishing spiritual qualities that can provide a healing balm for our out-of-balance lives. Although this kind of experience could happen at any time, day or night, it is not something that can simply be added to one's to-do list and squeezed in between finishing up at work and doing the grocery shopping. We experience this sort of connection only when we allow time for it, which is increasingly rare in our overscheduled lives. Yet we desperately need to *make* time for it, because the nourishment it gives is a crucial antidote to our frenzied lifestyle and to the culture that feeds our nonstop pace of life.

This book is about slowing down. It is a guide to reclaiming our lives from the tyranny of our to-do lists and bringing more of the deep inner resources we all possess into our everyday living. When we are feeling overwhelmed and out of control, it helps to know how to step away from busyness and get enough perspective to remember what our true priorities are. We have this sense of perspective within us. When the perpetual motion of trying to get things done makes us dizzy, it helps to know how to find stillness. We have this stillness within us. When we feel at the mercy of others' demands, it helps to know how to center ourselves and respond with clarity. We have this clarity within us. These are the kinds of resources that flow from the Deep River realm. This book is a guide for contacting the dimension of our being where these spiritual qualities live. It will explain what the Deep River is and why it is important—not only for ourselves but for all our relationships—and then offer practical tools for accessing this realm more regularly and opening to it more fully when it unexpectedly breaks through life's routines.

The program described in these pages draws from my more than twenty-five years of guiding women in my private psychotherapy practice, in individual coaching sessions, and in workshops for groups and organizations. Its principles are based on the Deep River groups I developed and have led for scores of women over the last decade. In this work, I have seen so many women who, due to their chronic busyness and the culture that feeds it, are cut off from essential aspects of themselves. They feel disconnected from their deeper feelings, their creative possibilities, spiritual sustenance, and the sense of depth and meaning that makes what they do with their time feel worthwhile. This disconnection from self tends to negatively influence relationships with partners, children, coworkers, friends, and other family members. Simply put, when we are out of touch with ourselves, we suffer, but our relationships also suffer. While many women intuitively recognize, as they race through the motions of life at breakneck speed and with little joy, that something is profoundly out of balance with how they are living, they often cannot accurately identify the cause of their dis-ease nor find effective remedies. Contact with the Deep River within is an antidote to this cut-off, fragmented experience of life. It opens our lives to greater meaning and contentment and our relationships to greater compassion and connection. And it gives a sense of spaciousness to the rhythms of life that our daily routine rarely affords.

Chapter One lays out the culturewide problem of "too much to do, too little time," how it affects us as women, and how we attempt solutions that often compound the problem. Chapter Two suggests an alternative solution and introduces the realm of the Deep River, filling in what it looks like and feels like and why it is so important to nurture contact with it. This chapter also explains why slowing down, which we all sense to be necessary but have such a hard time doing, is key to finding your spiritual center and touching the Deep River.

Chapter Three introduces three preliminary doorways to the Deep River realm: recognizing the power of the culture, getting support, and keeping a journal. These three pave the way for the six central practices that follow. Chapters Four through Nine present the

Deep River practices, the essential tools for integrating the Deep River realm into your daily life. The first two, taking "time-in" and making boundaries, address the *outer* obstacles to slowing down, providing ways to pause and restructure daily life so that you can dip down into the Deep River. You'll find practical ways to make better choices about your daily routine and how you spend your time. The next three practices, befriending feelings, taming self-expectations, and practicing presence, show you how to work with the *inner* obstacles to slowing down. You will learn how to get more comfortable with difficult emotions, lighten up on your expectations of yourself, and deal with the distracting inner chatter that can keep all of us from being truly present to the people we care about and the activities that make up our days. It's essential to address both the outer dimension and the inner dimension in order to be able to slow down and find your balance day to day. Integrating these two dimensions, the final practice, doing something you love, guides you to express yourself in the world, or "at the surface," in ways that arise out of and draw from the Deep River. When the inner and the outer are connected, we are tapped into the source of depth and meaning in our lives. The result is activity that is satisfying, renewing, and energizing rather than fragmenting and draining.

During my years of working with women who seek to connect with the Deep River, I've found that they need two other important types of tools: (1) tools to help them recognize what I call "blocking beliefs" and (2) exercises to help bring the concepts to life. Blocking beliefs are common mental and emotional assumptions we make that range from the seemingly benign ("I can't have fun until everything's checked off the list") to the more clearly self-damaging ("If I don't do it all perfectly, I'm a complete failure"). All of them block progress toward living a life of more balance, satisfaction, and depth. In each of the chapters on the Deep River practices, the "Blocking Beliefs" section will help you identify your own personal blocking beliefs, learn how to question or challenge them, and, if appropriate, replace them with more useful working assumptions.

The exercises, which can be done alone, with a friend, or in a group, are tools for initiating change in your day-to-day experience. They will give you insight and understanding about how the Deep River process works for you personally, as well as guide you toward *experiencing* the concepts so that you can make them your own. And sometimes the exercises are actually fun!

Finally, Chapter Ten broadens the lens through which the Deep River within is considered, taking it from the personal to the planetary, and discusses the implications of this work for our children, for our world, and for our future.

A Note About Reading This Book in a Group

Over the past twelve years of working with groups, I have been continually impressed by what participants teach one another through sharing their experiences. Chapter Three will talk more about the importance of getting support as you redefine your rhythms and routine in order to live a more balanced life. For now, let me just say this: you will benefit from reading this book and doing the exercises by yourself, but you will benefit even more if you can find a buddy to read the book with or even just to check in with periodically about the progress you're making. You will benefit the most if you can organize a group of friends or introduce the concept of the Deep River into an existing women's group so that you can read the book and do the exercises together. Not only will you gain from the wisdom of the group, but the mutual support will give you needed strength to counter the rapid currents of our culture.

However you choose to engage in the process of contacting the Deep River, may it be of benefit—to you and to all whose lives you touch.

"My life had started to feel so stagnant,
like it was atrophied. Everything shrunk down
to the roles I played. I had loved doing them, . . .
I really had, but they were drying up,
and they weren't really me. Do you understand?
I felt there had to be some other life beneath the one I had,
like an underground river or something,
and that I would die if I didn't dig down to it."
—Sue Monk Kidd

"How we spend our days is, of course,
how we spend our lives."
—Annie Dillard

Part One

Thirsting for the Deep River Realm

When I introduce something new into my life, I find it helpful to understand as much as I can about what I'm dealing with; perhaps this is true for you, too. When my mind has a good grasp of why it makes sense to do something, I am more motivated to actually do it. This is the purpose of Part One. The first chapter provides an understanding of what it takes to slow down and find our way to the Deep River in a fast-paced culture that is focused on the superficial, yet thirsting for depth. The second chapter gives a fuller description of the Deep River realm, the rationale for going there, and a map of the Deep River process. Once you are equipped with an understanding of the Deep River realm, Chapter Three gets you started and shows you ways of using the material ahead in order to make it easier, more effective, and more enjoyable.

Chapter One

The Disease of A-Thousand-Things-To-Do

> It has always seemed obvious to me that the
> faster I move, the more things I can do and the
> more fun and meaning my life will have. But it
> has gotten to the point where my days, crammed
> with all sorts of activities, feel like an Olympic
> endurance event: the everydayathon.
> —*Jay Walljasper*, Utne Magazine

When my children were two and five, I remember thinking, "I'm pretty sure I used to have an inner life. What happened to it?" Most days, I was experiencing life in a way shared by almost every woman I met.[1] I later came to call this experience "life as to-do list." Here are some of its characteristics:

- Rushing
- *Feeling* in a rush, whether there is a reason to rush or not
- Never having quite enough time
- Too many demands on too little time
- Too many interruptions while trying to meet those demands
- Skidding across the surface of life, checking things off the ever-present, never-ending List, perhaps getting things done, but going through the motions in a fragmented way, without feeling any sense of satisfaction or completion before having to push on to whatever's next

- Feeling disconnected, in the midst of this everydayathon, from the *meaning* of what I am doing, from myself, and from the people I care about

This experience often includes feeling exhausted, overwhelmed, and stressed; it sometimes includes feeling empty, numb, and depressed; and it seldom includes feeling a sense of joy, contentment, fun, or gratitude for the simple pleasures of life.

Does any of this sound familiar?

Based on my private therapy practice and my group work with women during the last decade, I would say this experience is far too common. We feel its effects viscerally, in physical ailments that range from migraines, hypertension, and heart disease to gastrological disorders like ulcers, irritable bowel syndrome, and colitis.[2] We feel its effects emotionally, sometimes in clinically diagnosed depression and anxiety.[3] We may try to remedy the effects with prescribed medications (women receive two-thirds of the prescriptions for tranquilizers and antidepressants in the United States)[4] or through self-medication with alcohol or other substances, including food, tobacco, and illicit drugs.[5]

Jennifer, a woman in one of my Deep River groups, is a stay-at-home mom with four young children. She came to the group because the demands of caring for her home and family left her feeling as if she were "coming apart at the seams." Her goal in joining the group was to be able to do what needed to get done without being so frantic. "I feel as if I'm always under the gun, always hurrying to get the next thing done. At the end of the day, I'm exhausted, but I can't really relax." The hardest time of day for Jennifer was in the evening, from dinnertime through her children's bedtime. Her only relief from the pressure she felt was her glass or two—or three—of wine in the evening. This "solution" did relax her, but it also made her a bit foggy, which in turn made it more difficult for her to get her kids to bed on time. She would stay up later to compensate and then have a tough time getting up when she wanted to the next morning, thus reinforcing her sense that she was always under the gun.

Whether we seem to be handling our busy lives well or are experiencing physical or emotional symptoms and using some sort of mood-altering substance to ease the pressure, most of us can feel trapped by the tyranny of our to do's. Once we reach a certain degree of overwhelm, we may look for help or try to make a change. When Melissa, one of my clients, hired a professional organizer to help her with the clutter in her home, just finding a time when both she and the organizer were free to meet was a task in itself! At first, Melissa was excited about getting her piles of papers cleared up and organized and having a system for keeping them that way. But the effect was short-lived. Shifting her habits, sorting her mail and other papers in new ways, and putting them in new places became overwhelming tasks in themselves.

It is often the case that our best efforts at getting organized or simplifying our lives don't bring a lasting shift. When we fail in our attempts to rearrange or simplify daily routines, self-confidence can suffer. We begin to wonder, "What is wrong with *me*?"

The Fallacy of "What Is Wrong with Me?"

Most women are quite skilled at blaming themselves. When my second child was born, I was surprised at the quantum leap in stress I began to experience in my role as mother. Juggling work, the needs of a baby and a three-year-old, and keeping the household running left me feeling ragged at the edges. Despite some help from my husband, baby-sitters, and a flexible work schedule, I felt overwhelmed by all the characteristics of "life as to-do list." I kept thinking, "How do single moms do it? How do women who have three or four or five kids do it? How do women with no job flexibility do it? How does my neighbor, who seems to manage everything so effortlessly, also have time to bake bread?" And that wondering led me to ask what seemed a logical next question: "What is wrong with *me*?!"

In trying to answer this question, I'd analyze which personal traits, flaws, and shortcomings might be causing my stressed and fragmented experience of daily life. I'd wonder, "Is it because the world is divided into two groups—the organized and the unorganized—and by accident of birth, I fall into the latter category? Is it because I'm a Gemini, astrological sign of the twins, which destines me to forever divide my attention between at least two things at once?" Or I would think, "Maybe the experience of mothering young children, which easily qualifies as boot camp in how to never do anything for more than five minutes without being interrupted, has permanently altered some brain cells. Or maybe it's the fact that my desire to please makes me too willing to interrupt myself to respond to others' needs. Maybe I'm just not determined enough, or tough enough." The fretting and speculation went on and on.

Now, many years later, I know that this self-blaming tendency is very common. Women see themselves as not organized enough, not smart enough, not disciplined enough, not efficient enough, not focused enough, not good enough at parenting, at communicating, at relaxing, at making choices . . . not good enough, period. I also now understand that the belief underlying most of this self-criticism is "something is wrong with me."

Meditation teacher Tara Brach calls the state created by this belief the "trance of unworthiness."[6] Much like the seemingly scripted drama of a bad dream, our actions in this trance state are defined and driven by a fear of not measuring up. It is as if "the rest of the world is merely a backdrop as we struggle to get somewhere, to be a better person, to accomplish, to avoid making mistakes."[7] In her book *Radical Acceptance*, Brach tells the story of a meditation student's experience that awakened her to the tragedy of living in this trance:

> Marilyn had spent many hours sitting at the bedside of her dying mother—reading to her, meditating next to her late at night, holding her hand and telling her over and over that she loved her. Most of the time, Marilyn's mother remained unconscious, her breath labored and erratic. One morning before dawn, she suddenly opened her eyes and looked clearly and intently at her daughter. "You know," she whispered softly, "all my life I thought something was wrong with me."

Shaking her head slightly, as if to say, "What a waste," she closed her eyes and drifted back into a coma. Several hours later she passed away.[8]

Her mother's dying words were a wake-up call for Marilyn, help-ing her break out of her own trance of unworthiness: "It was her parting gift. I realized I didn't have to lose my life in the same way that she did. Out of love—for my mother, for life—I resolved to hold myself with more acceptance and kindness."[9]

Living in a trance of unworthiness, with the underlying belief that something is wrong with you has at least two unfortunate effects. First, it prevents you from seeing and appreciating all that you *are* doing. One evening in my early years of child rearing, I took to my journal in sheer frustration after one of those all-too-frequent marathon bedtime routines. I simply made a list of everything I had done that day. It included lots of very mundane tasks like laundry, grocery shopping, making dinner. I listed everything I could think of. There was nothing momentous on the list, but I actually felt quite a sense of accomplishment when I read it. Somehow, seeing on paper what was filling my days silenced, at least for a time, the inner voice that kept saying I never did enough.

The other negative effect of the something-is-wrong-with-me syndrome is that it drives us to do *more* in order to try to be better, keeping us on the very treadmill that has us feeling overwhelmed and inadequate to begin with. If feeling inadequate causes us to add more self-improvement activities to our list, we reinforce the pattern of overdoing, which further strengthens our sense of inadequacy. There is no shortage of people and programs telling us how to improve our-selves, but if these opportunities start with the assumption that there is something wrong with us, the solution will inevitably become part of the problem. In my groups, I sometimes share a cartoon by Dan Wasserman of a frazzled-looking woman doing an exercise routine. The caption reads, "I exercise strenuously for longevity . . . stretch for flexibility, meditate for tranquility . . . count fat, eat right, rest well, brush, floss, warm up, cool down . . . no wonder I don't have a life!"[10]

The truth is that personal inadequacy is not the root of the problem. In fact, we are all asking the wrong question. Instead of asking, "What is wrong with *me?*" as we try not to sink under the pressure of our to-do lists, we should be asking, "What is wrong with *this picture?*"

The Water We Swim In

While our personal history, habits, and shortcomings do play a part in our fragmented sense of daily life, we need to zoom out and see the picture from a wider angle. There are larger influences at work in our feelings of overwhelm. They're not personal to you, to me, or to any of us, but they shape our experience unless we become aware of them and learn to resist. These influences constitute an all-encompassing environment, like the air we breathe or like water we swim in. They are all around us, even within us; they emanate from our *culture*.

The culture we live in, with its ever-expanding array of technological advances and time-saving conveniences, is beginning to feel more like a nightmare in which we are getting nowhere fast than the dream of comfort, leisure, and freedom we set out to create. Newspaper and magazine articles, books, and talks about how to simplify, slow down, and calm down are more and more common. Yoga classes provide serious competition in the exercise market, where hard-driving aerobics once reigned. Meditation, an activity on the fringe of American society thirty years ago, was the cover story of an issue of *Time* magazine in 2003 and was featured in a 2004 issue of *Newsweek* as part of a series of articles called "The New Science of Mind and Body." As a society, we are beginning to wake up to a profound imbalance in the way we conduct our lives, but we are still so deeply and unconsciously embedded in a culture of speed, interruption, and distraction that it's difficult to fully see or feel its effects, much less counter them in any significant way.

For the last several years, I've been collecting newspaper and magazine articles that address the issues of speed and lack of time and what we can do about them. Some articles have insightful analyses of the problem. Some have useful suggestions about how to slow down and simplify, and some offer examples of people who have effectively downsized and created a simpler lifestyle. The fact that we find these topics newsworthy indicates that the water we swim in has a rapid current indeed.

The articles I find the most fascinating and amusing are the ones that offer "solutions" without so much as touching the problem. For example, a popular women's magazine featured a brief (so as to be read *quickly!*) article called "Hurry Up and Relax" that was inadvertently laugh-aloud funny. The first line reads, "If you run yourself ragged rushing through the day and find no time to put on the brakes, don't despair: you may not have to slow down to relax."[11] Another popular health magazine devoted its cover story to suggestions on how to "simplify your life and *finally* have free time." One suggestion is a group of recipes for "warp-speed weeknight meals" that allow one to "forget cooking." Another suggests that rather than reading books to stay "hip to the latest best-sellers," one might just read the reviews to get the highlights; that will "see you through any casual conversation, and provide ready-made commentary to boot."[12] No need to bother with the pesky, time-consuming task of actually reading a book!

Once again, we might ask, "What is wrong with this picture?" These articles that attempt to tell us how to slow down without slowing down or how to save time at any cost are symptoms of our inability to really grasp the underlying problem and its pervasiveness. These so-called solutions do not question their culture-based assumptions.

As we try to find new ways to cut corners and pare down the time it takes to do everything from making meals to tending our relationships, we fail to notice that we are operating on the assumption, a fundamental and dearly held one in our society, that faster is automatically better. We usually don't pay attention to the fact that, unlike a hundred years ago, when the pace of life was set by the rhythms of nature, the pace of our days is set by our technology: cars, planes, cell phones, computers, the rapid-fire images of television, and so on. When I learned from my son that computer technology is based on the nanosecond, or a billionth of a second, my first thought was "What *is* a billionth of a second?" And then, more important, "What does it mean for the pace of our lives that we live in an age that has a name for an increment of time that is a billionth of a second?"

The strange irony in our sped-up lives is the fact that while our technology has enabled us to get things done faster and faster, we seem to have less and less time. Women I meet complain almost universally that they don't have enough time. "Our lives are filled with devices invented to 'save time,'" explains author and columnist Michael Ventura, but "these devices don't really save time; they merely shorten tasks. A task that took hours now may take only minutes . . . but those hours aren't 'saved'; instead, they are used for other tasks that take only minutes. . . . What we have is a staccato rhythm of doing one thing after another after another, filling up the 'saved' time with new chores, and what we experience is . . . a frustrated sense of continual interruption."[13] As we will see in Chapter Two, our sense of time is subjective, malleable, and to some extent culture-bound, and the experience of "not enough hours in the day" goes along with a linear sense of time that is chopped into small increments, making for the unsatisfying staccato rhythm that Ventura describes.

Adding to our pressured sense of time is our acceptance of the constant interruptions that punctuate our days. Most of us don't question the inevitability of being interrupted by phone calls as we go about our daily activities; often the interruption itself is interrupted by another call. (And we actually *pay* to have this privilege!) A woman in one of my groups had an epiphany when she realized that she could cancel the call-waiting option on her phone service. She said that it somehow hadn't occurred to her that she had a choice about this source of interruption and that she could choose to eliminate it.

Along with speed and interruption, distraction is a fundamental characteristic of the cultural water we swim in. When Edward Hallowell, a doctor who specializes in the treatment of attention deficit disorder (ADD), was asked about the high incidence of

ADD in the United States, part of his answer was to describe what has been called "pseudo-ADD," or "attention deficit trait."[14] According to Hallowell, this ailment mimics the symptoms of the neurological disorder but is environmentally induced, and affects a significant portion of the population. Essentially, he is saying that many of us are being driven to distraction (the title of his book about ADD) not by a genetic disorder but by the very culture in which we live. New research confirms this, showing that children ages one to three who watch two or more hours of television a day have a harder time paying attention by age seven than those who are exposed to little or no television early in life.[15]

I remember being shocked the first time I saw someone wheeling a cart through a grocery store while talking on a cell phone. Now I am disturbed by the fact that I am no longer shocked. People everywhere are driving while talking on the phone, talking on the phone while working at a computer, working on a computer while eating, eating while watching TV while doing homework in front of a computer while on the phone. We now have a word for this distracted behavior—*multitasking*—that makes it seem desirable and praiseworthy. Our culture seems to direct us to do too many things at once, and the quality of our family and social lives, our work lives, and our inner lives is suffering deeply. By way of example, here are some observations:

- The average working couple in America spends twenty minutes a day together.

- "Family time" has become a goal, an achievement, rather than a natural consequence of being a family.

- Many of the families who are not frenzied and exhausted by trying to make enough money to keep food on the table are equally exhausted and trapped in a cycle of overwork and overconsumption.

- Dropping in on a neighbor, commonplace just thirty or forty years ago, is an almost nonexistent social behavior.

- Keeping busy and multitasking are unquestioned as praise-worthy behaviors. Slowing down, doing one thing at a time, and taking our time to do it, is becoming a lost art in America.

- As a society, we are reading less. Computer technology is supplanting the written word. Sven Birkerts, author of *The Gutenberg Elegies*, makes the case that with the decline of print, we are, as a culture, becoming shallower, that we "are giving up on wisdom, the struggle for which has for millennia been central to the very idea of culture."[16]

So once we see that there *is* something wrong with our cultural picture and not necessarily with us individually, what can we do about it? Is it possible to follow a different path, take some measure of control, and downshift in our own lives, even if the world around us continues on the fast track? My answer is "yes," and the rest of this book explains how to go about doing it.

✿ Exercise: The "What I *Have* Done" List

A list of things to do is a reminder of what we *haven't* done and can reinforce a sense of inadequacy and never doing enough. In this brief exercise, the focus is on what you have already accomplished, so that you can experience the cup as half full instead of half empty in relation to the ever-present to-do list.

At the end of a day, make a list of everything you've done that day. Write down everything you can think of, including things you think don't count, like shuttling your kids around, showering, or making a phone call that only took a couple of minutes. When you're finished, read over your what-I-*have*-done list, take a deep breath, and appreciate yourself.

You can make this other kind of list any time you become aware that your to-do list is triggering you to ask, "What is wrong with me?"

———

༃ Exercise: Registering the Pace of Your Life

Next time you are driving on the highway, drive five miles per hour more slowly than you usually do for at least five minutes. Notice how you feel. Are you more relaxed? More restless? First one, and then the other? Just notice what it feels like to slow down your ordinary pace.

Driving is only one of the many activities in which you may be unconsciously matching a pace that is faster than you need or want to go. You can try this intentional slowing down with walking— even just from one room to another—eating, or almost any daily activity.

This simple exercise is intended to heighten awareness of the external pressure to speed up and the internal tendency to match the pace of our surroundings. Heightened awareness of the effect of your environment is valuable because you are more likely to make positive choices in relation to the culture of speed once you can actually feel its effects.

With the recognition that our culture's need for speed rather than our own shortcomings is at the root of our problems of fragmentation, time pressure, and trying to do too much, let's take a look at where the solution lies.

Chapter Two

The Deep River Within

In the face of "too much" we gradually become dry,
our hearts get tired, our energies become spare,
and a mysterious longing for—we almost never
have a name for it other than "a something"—
rises up in us more and more.
—*Clarissa Pinkola Estés,*
Women Who Run with the Wolves

When we get the urge to simplify and slow down, most of us tend to think, "I just need to get more organized." Although time management might be helpful, it can also be one of those "solutions" that is part of the problem: we manage our time better so that we can more efficiently pack more activity into our already overpacked schedule.

My view, and the approach of this book, is that we need to look in an entirely different, perhaps unfamiliar direction for a solution to the sense of overwhelm. To regain our balance and find meaning and satisfaction in how we live, we need to "drop down" and look beneath the perpetual-motion busyness of our daily lives.

From Surface to Depth

When I speak of looking beneath or dropping down, I am talking about moving from a more outward focus at the surface of our lives to a more inward focus deep within ourselves. The Deep River Diagram (see page 22) illustrates this movement. We can move from surface to depth, or outer to inner, because we all have a place of depth within us, whether or not we are aware of it at any given time. This place of depth might be thought of as the spiritual dimension within us. There are many names for this inner realm and probably as many different experiences of it as there are people. Some describe it as "going home"; for some, it is the place for contact with the "still, small voice" within; others say it is where they go in themselves to reconnect with God, with meaning, or with a sense of the big picture of their life or for spiritual renewal or for creative inspiration. When I drop down or go inside, I often have the image of an underground river that is always there, always flowing through me, from a source beyond me, carrying deeply nourishing, life-giving qualities. After I first saw the Deep River in my mind's eye, I discovered that it is not my image alone. Jungian analyst and author Clarissa Estés writes of the *rio abajo rio*, "the river beneath the river, which flows and flows into our lives."[1] May Sarton writes of the "deep still water" where dreams and images live.[2] When Jessie, the main character in Sue Monk Kidd's *The Mermaid Chair*, longed for a more authentic, satisfying life, she described the feeling that "there had to be some other life beneath the one I had, like an underground river or something, and that I would die if I didn't dig down to it."[3]

My name for this place of depth is the Deep River within. We all have this dimension within us, but we differ in what we find there as well as how we experience it. Janine, a woman in one of my groups, describes her experience in this straightforward way: "When I go there, time slows down, I get clarity, and the self-talk tape shuts off." Another group member refers to the Psalm celebrating "the secret place of the Most High" to help her orient herself toward the Deep River realm. She says, "I tend to think of the Deep River as the place where the noise stops and a sense of peace and stillness finally takes over. It's the place where I *feel* rather than *think* my true nature." Another woman describes it as "where I disconnect from the chatter so that I can connect to what is real for me, what makes my heart sing, what pains me, and what is important to me."

Of course, the Deep River is not a physical destination. A favorite corner of the living room or an especially beautiful natural setting might be conducive to tapping into the Deep River realm, but the Deep River is a state of consciousness rather than an actual place.

Marie, a graphic designer, finds that drawing brings her to the Deep River within:

> When I am drawing and relaxed it feels like I am in a tunnel where there are no distractions around me. I am not aware of my body at all or anyone or anything, for that matter. My sense of time is suspended, and I am deeply concentrated. I trust that my hand "knows" and that I need to get out of the way to allow it to just move and feel and not direct it. This is not easy to do, because my mind and judgment often get in the way. But when it does work, it is a very relaxed and deeply satisfying state.

Deep River Qualities

While everyone's experience of the Deep River state is different, certain qualities are often described—for example,

- Peace, calm
- Silence, stillness
- Aliveness, vitality
- Gratitude, grace
- Clarity, perspective
- Creativity, inspiration
- Joy, contentment
- Fluidity, ease
- Trusting, letting go
- Tenderness, love
- Groundedness, solidity

- Wholeness, sense of self
- Universality, sense of connection to others
- Compassion, for one's own and others' suffering

This is not a comprehensive list. One or more of these qualities, or perhaps something not listed, might describe your experience of contact with the Deep River realm. Don't be surprised if this contact has a bittersweet quality; our deepest experiences often contain a poignant mixture of light and dark, joy and sorrow. The exercise at the end of this chapter is designed to take you to your own experience of what I am describing here, whatever its particular qualities are for you.

In Deep River experiences, one's sense of time is almost always altered. Janine says that time slows down, and Marie says that her sense of time is suspended. Another woman says that time "opens up," while another says, "I feel when I am in this place that I have all the time in the world." These comments reflect the reality that our sense of time is subjective and malleable. When we are totally absorbed in something—a creative endeavor or a conversation with a friend—what seemed like a half hour can actually turn out to be two or three. In the Deep River realm, time is not experienced as linear, constraining, and stressful the way it often is in the rest of our lives. Rather, we have a sense of timelessness or spaciousness. Time, or lack of it, ceases to be the enemy. That is why, as we'll see in later chapters, we need to look toward the Deep River within to find balance in our harried lives: perhaps it actually isn't more time that we need but a different way of experiencing the time we have.

The Value of the Deep River

Some of you reading this chapter may recognize the Deep River realm as familiar territory. Others may be wondering, "What is this for *me*?" or "Even if I assume I have a place of depth within me, how do I find it?" Having questions like these does *not* mean that something is wrong with you. Our prevailing culture neither teaches us about nor values this inner realm, much less shows us how to gain access to it. The coming chapters will describe *how* we make contact with the Deep River, but first we need to understand *why* this contact is important.

Clarissa Estés describes what happens when we are cut off from our inner selves through the archetypal story of the seal woman, which is told in many northern countries throughout the world. The water is the seal woman's home, what we might call her place of depth. Although she belongs to the sea and lives beneath the water as a seal, at night she can take human form. One night, she and her seal sisters shed their pelts and dance naked atop a rock by the sea. A lonely man comes upon them and steals the seal woman's pelt before she can put it back on and slip back into the sea. He pleads with her to be his wife. Estés says of the pelt, "[It] is not so much an article as the representation of a feeling state and a state of being—one that is cohesive, soulful, and of the wildish female nature. When a woman is in this state, she feels entirely in and of herself."[4] And being without the pelt "causes a woman to pursue what she thinks she should do, rather than what she truly wishes."[5]

The seal woman agrees to remain with the lonely man, but when she stays too long on land, away from the depths, without her pelt, she begins to dry out. Her skin cracks, her hair thins, she begins to limp, and her eyes lose their moisture. This dried-out state, "peeling, limping, losing juice, going blind"[6] is a good metaphorical description of what happens when we have no access to our own depths. Our lives seem flat, dry, and empty, even if they are full of activity, people, and things. We feel as if we are going through the motions of life, but not really living.

The seal woman's overly long stay on land points to another effect of being cut off from our deeper nature: we are more prone to physical symptoms of stress, to addictive behavior, to conflict and disconnection in our relationships, to dissatisfaction in our work and in our lives. We need to be able to find our way back to our water home for replenishment and renewal. In the story, when the seal woman finally breaks free from the man, reclaims her pelt, and returns to the sea, the shine returns to her hair and eyes, her sight is restored, and her body becomes plump and full and strong again. Access to the deeper realms within us gives back us our juice, our vital energy and resilience. We return to our true selves, or in Estés's language, we return to home and to being wholly in our skin, which in turn can help us relate more fully and openly to others and to the activities we engage in. We find a sense of connection to something larger than our own individual concerns and a sense of meaning that makes what we do with our time feel worthwhile.

Janet, a young mother of two, experienced the value of contact with the Deep River when she began to take time each day to, in her words, "find [her] deeper self" and to practice staying in touch with her depth in the midst of her daily interactions. She said, "If I approach relationships from that deeper place instead of the more superficial place, I'm more *responsible*—not *responsible* in the sense of taking charge but more *responsible* in the sense of able to respond." As an example, she described a typical afternoon when her son was sitting in the next room doing some homework:

> I was rushing around the kitchen like a chicken with its head cut off, cleaning, with a sense of urgency. My son asked me a question; he wanted my attention. My tendency is to say, "When I'm done," and continue with a sense of urgency. So at first, I said, "In a little while," and then I had an awareness, because I'm practicing this, that I was very revved up. I noticed it in my body, all this tension and unnecessary movement, and I made an effort to quiet my body. Then my mind got more quiet, and I said, "Yeah, I'll be right there. I can do this a little later." I went in with a sense of calm and quiet, and I was able to really connect with him in a way that was relaxing and fulfilling for both of us. I know that's what he wanted: to connect with me—with *me*, not that person who was cleaning counters with urgency.

As an afterthought, she said, "By the way, there was no urgency, really. It was just a *sense* of urgency, the sense that nothing will ever be done, the sense of 'What is going to happen if I stop now, for 15 minutes, when I have to finish cleaning the kitchen, put in a load of laundry, blah, blah, blah?' That's the so-called urgency!"

After she described her experience, Janet said, "It's even better, because when I went back to cleaning the counters, I could remember why I was doing it. I remembered what all this is for; it's for the family." As she said this, Janet began to tear up. In describing this interaction, she seemed to recognize what truly mattered to her. She said, "It's really about coming from that place of loving, and the doing gets in the way of the loving, but we just don't see that most of the time. And all of the doing is *because* of the loving, but it gets in the way." Then she added, "There's so much tenderness in that deep place that we don't have access to so much of the time."

Visualizing the Deep River Process

Janet's experience demonstrates the effect that dropping down can have on life at the surface. Of course, sometimes urgency is real and we can't take time to sit down and talk with our children. But often, especially in a cultural context that values speed and doing, we, like Janet, stay at the surface of our lives, keeping busy with a false sense of urgency and missing opportunities to engage in fulfilling ways with those we love or with ourselves or even with a mundane task such as cleaning the counter.

So how do we gain access to and draw on the inner resources that bring deep nourishment or "juice," as Estés puts it, to our ordinary lives? I developed the Deep River Diagram over many years of working with women to help them visualize both the process and the essential tools necessary to open up access to the Deep River. As I've said before, touching the depth within us is not something we can simply add to our to-do list or squeeze in as we go from one errand to another. The Deep River realm may unexpectedly break through life's routines, but more often, we have to exert conscious effort to create the conditions that open us to this dimension. There may be some cultures in which people can more easily drop down and touch the Deep River, but in our culture of speed, interruption, and distraction, we will remain at the surface unless we make a conscious effort.

Women in my groups have used the Deep River Diagram as a reminder that it *is* possible to slow down and connect with what matters. They keep a copy of it in their datebook, post it next to their computer, or tape it to their refrigerator or dashboard. One group member says, "I have a copy of the diagram taped to a wall along with some favorite sayings, near where I meditate. I put it there because I love the concept of 'dropping down' that's embodied in it and because it's a clear reminder of what it is I'm working on."

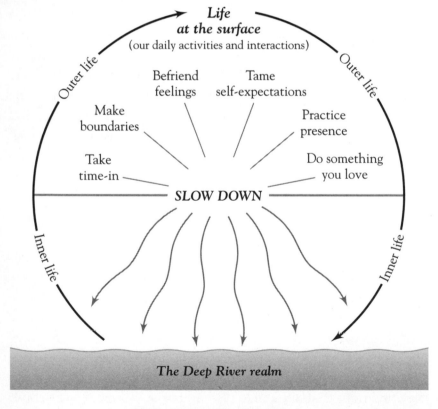

The Deep River Diagram

The Key: Slowing Down

In the center of the diagram, in large letters, are the words *Slow down*. At least in twenty-first-century North America, this is the most fundamental prerequisite for receiving nourishment from the Deep River within. To see the importance of slowing down, consider this brief exercise:

Imagine a beautiful summer garden in full bloom on a sunny day, with all the colors and scents, shapes and textures of a variety of flowers and shrubs. Take a moment right now to picture this garden, however you see it in your mind's eye. Imagine wandering through it on a winding path, perhaps stopping now and gazing at whichever flowers you are drawn to. Notice the colors and shapes of the flowers you are looking at. Imagine that you can breathe in the colors and breathe in the beauty you see, just as you might be breathing in the scent. Notice what happens in your body as you imagine inhaling this beauty.

Now, imagine that you are driving in a car at sixty miles an hour. Off to your right is a beautiful summer garden in full bloom on a sunny day. Oops, it's gone by. Did you catch it? You might notice a blur of color before it's gone, and you might tell others that you saw a beautiful garden while you were driving, but there is simply no way that you can truly take in the garden's beauty, let it touch you, and be nourished by it while speeding by at sixty miles an hour.

Despite what our faster-is-better culture may tell us, we *do* need to slow down if we want to open up access to the Deep River within. There is no question that this can be difficult; a habitually fast pace has its own momentum that is hard to break. If we're used to living in overdrive, slowing down may be hard to tolerate; we may feel uncomfortable, unproductive, bored, or restless at a slower pace. If it's uncomfortable, we may not stop until we encounter life events that *throw* us off the treadmill, forcing us to slow down at least temporarily, which can result in opening us up to depth.

For Louise, a mother of two who worked full-time, the event that shifted her life dramatically happened to someone she was close to. Louise had worked hard for fifteen years at a job in sales and marketing, which, she said, "sucked the life right out of me." Looking back at her life then, Louise described it as "totally externally focused, driven, and very out of control." During that time, one of Louise's friends was in a very severe car accident, and it was unclear whether she would survive. During one of the first nights that her friend was in the hospital, Louise slept only intermittently, thinking and dreaming about her and her family for what seemed like most of the night. She said, "Toward morning, just as I was awakening— I was no longer sleeping but I really was not awake, either—I had this thought about my friend: 'Even if her life is over now, she can *know* that she has done a great job as a mother.' Then all of a sudden, I applied that thought to myself, and I remember the clutching feeling in my chest. It was a visceral reaction as I thought: 'If I were to die tomorrow, that couldn't be said about me.'" She saw that she had been so distracted by her job that she wasn't living her values, which to her meant putting her children first. The incongruity between what she believed in and how she was living was so stark and jolting to her in that moment that she had to act. "I gave my notice at a job that I'd had for fifteen years; I didn't go for options; I didn't think about how else I might resolve this. It was completely, 'I've got to stop this freight train, and get off.'"

The next several months were hard in a different way for Louise. She was at home and spending much more time with her children, but she still felt driven and could not settle down. "I was sewing pillow covers with a vengeance! I felt enormous stress, but now most of it was self-generated." Eventually, in an effort to address the stress she was feeling both physically and emotionally, Louise attended a weekend retreat that included some guided visualization. At first, she had trouble focusing her attention inward, but on one of the inner journeys, she found herself able to truly go inside, and her inner world opened up. She went in her mind's eye back to her childhood home, and reconnected with a deep sense of loneliness that had been with her often as a child. She realized that in her adult life, the "freight train" energy that caused her so much stress was fueled in part by trying to avoid the old feeling of discomfort with quiet aloneness from her childhood. This awareness helped her with the changes she wanted to make. Later, she said, "I had lived my life for so long in an outer fashion, and I was so out of sync and so screwed up. I had some sense that I needed to look inside, but it was so hard. I didn't know how to do it."

Her weekend retreat was the beginning of an inner exploration that led Louise to one of my groups, among other things, and eventually, as her children got older, to an entirely new career that connects back to that early-morning moment that affected her so profoundly: she teaches and writes about parenting skills. "What I'm doing now uses all of who I am: my professional experience, my skill, my education. And it's married to my passion. So it's very powerful for me. And now, because what I'm doing is inner-driven, there's an energy and an authenticity about it that keeps me going."

Sadly, the norms of our nonstop way of life mean that one of the most frequently traveled paths to the Deep River is through crisis—a serious illness, the death of a loved one, divorce, or some other major loss. Whether they happen to ourselves or, as in Louise's case, to someone close to us, such events stop us in our tracks, prompting us to look inward. The premise of this book is that we don't have to wait until we are in shock or in terrible pain to begin to find our way to the depth within. We can intentionally, consciously create conditions that invite the Deep River to flow into our lives.

Dropping Down and Returning to the Surface

Encircling the Deep River Diagram are two arrows that represent the movement we are seeking to create in our day-to-day living, from surface to depth and back to the surface again. The goal of this book is not to encourage retreating to a cave or monastery to live out our days in silence. Rather, the goal is to establish a consistent rhythm within our daily routine that allows us to tap into the Deep

River, draw nourishment from it, and return to life at the surface with renewed perspective and vitality, remembering what really matters to us. In this way, what we do in our outer life (our daily activities and interactions) is informed by our inner life and gives expression to the qualities of the Deep River realm.

As I write this, it's winter in New England. Last week, nature provided a regionwide enforced slowdown in the form of a blizzard. In the days after the storm, several of my clients described having spent their snow day at a slower pace, taking time off, doing things they ordinarily would not have taken time for. My own sense of the day was one of unburdened spaciousness, as if the yoke of time had been temporarily lifted off of me and everyone around me. Aside from shoveling snow, the weather forced a kind of Sabbath, a day of rest. The cycle of activity, rest, and return is crucial to being able to maintain balance and energy in our lives, yet, short of a blizzard or another motion-stopping event, we override and push past the rest part of the cycle again and again. The poet May Sarton writes of this need for rest and the tendency to override it in her *Journal of a Solitude*:

> A strange empty day. I did not feel well; lay around, looked at daffodils against the white walls. . . . I always forget how important the empty days are, how important it may be sometimes not to expect to produce anything, even a few lines in a journal. I am still pursued by a neurosis about work inherited from my father. A day where one has not pushed oneself to the limit seems a damaged damaging day, a sinful day. Not so! The most valuable thing we can do for the psyche, occasionally, is to let it rest, wander, live in the changing light of a room, not try to be or do anything whatever. Tonight I do feel in a state of grace, limbered up, less strained.[7]

Sarton is describing the renewing effect of stepping out of the habitual mode of produce, produce, produce and allowing one's whole being to pause. I will talk more about this in Chapter Four. For now, I simply want to highlight the importance of the cycle that the arrows in the diagram represent. That cycle of activity, dropping down, and return is the antithesis of what has been so aptly named our 24/7 way of life.

The Practices

Above the words *Slow down* on the diagram are six radiating lines, each with the name of one of the six essential tools or practices for opening access to the Deep River realm. These tools have a reciprocal relationship to slowing down—that is, slowing down makes it easier to do each practice, and doing each practice helps us to slow down. These tools will be explained in detail in the next several chapters. In brief, they are as follows:

1. *Take time-in:* Learn to gather energy and find balance by taking uninterrupted alone time to drop below the surface of daily activity.

2. *Make boundaries:* Learn the primary skill for heading off the feeling of being overwhelmed: saying "no."

3. *Befriend feelings:* Learn to accept and make friends with uncomfortable feelings that you may be trying to avoid by keeping busy.

4. *Tame self-expectations:* Learn to lighten up and take the self-critical voice of perfectionism less seriously.

5. *Practice presence:* Learn to address *mental* busyness by cultivating mindfulness of the present moment.

6. *Do something you love:* Learn to create time to experience the renewing power of doing something simply for the enjoyment of doing it.

As the arrows in the lower half of the diagram indicate, each of these six practices, in combination with slowing down, is a potential doorway to the Deep River dimension. In addition, there are three preliminary practices designed to help you get started: recognizing the power of the culture, getting support, and keeping a journal. We'll be discussing these three tools in depth in the next chapter, and you'll begin to see how all of the practices fit together.

⟨⟩ Exercise: Reliving a Deep River Experience

Before we move on to the specific practices for connecting with the Deep River within, I encourage you to take a few moments to do a guided visualization exercise that will help you experience the inner realm that I have been talking about. I have found that we all have some experience of the Deep River dimension, even if we haven't tapped into it for weeks, months, or years. This exercise helps you remember one of these times and reconnect with the body sensations, feelings, and thoughts that accompany it. Reliving a positive experience of your inner nature can provide motivation to invite more contact with this dimension in your daily life. Reconnecting with your experience of the Deep River is important, too, because *experience* is the most valuable of all tools for slowing down and reclaiming your life.

To get the most from the exercise, find a place and time in which you will be undisturbed. You won't need a lot of time; even ten minutes of uninterrupted time is enough. Read through the exercise first. The words are meant to guide you toward an inner experience that is beyond words. They are only guidelines; you don't have to follow them exactly. After you have read through the exercise, do it at your own pace.

You can also have a friend read the exercise to you slowly, with some pauses to allow you to contact your experience. Take time to make some notes, if you wish, before you reciprocate and guide your friend through the exercise.

Close your eyes. Sit comfortably in a chair and consciously relax your body. Imagine your muscles loosening and let go of any tension you may be holding in them. Take a few moments to focus your attention on your breathing; allow the rhythm of your breath to quiet you and help focus your attention inside yourself.

Now, think of a time when you might have touched the Deep River. It might have been a time when you felt very energized or very calmed by being in nature or when you felt a sense of wonder at the natural world. Or it might have been an experience of being awed by something beautiful or an experience of communion with another person or with God or just a sense of a loving presence, some force larger than yourself that you were part of. It might have been an experience of deep connection to others—and to our common humanity—through either a shared grief or a shared joy. It might have been a time when you experienced a very clear insight about something troubling you or about how life works or the meaning of your life, or a time when you felt gratitude for simply being alive. Or it might have been an experience of being "in the flow" while doing some activity or a time when you felt somehow very fully yourself, very whole, fully alive. (Don't be surprised if what you remember is from a difficult time in your life. Sometimes we open more fully to life and to a greater depth within ourselves during painful or challenging times.)

Take your time to allow a memory of this experience to present itself. There is no one right experience. It could be something that happened very recently or an event from way back in your childhood. It could be an experience you had during an ordinary everyday activity, like washing the dishes, or one that happened during an important life event, like giving birth.

When you think of a time when you had this heightened awareness, make it as vivid as possible in your imagination. Allow yourself to relive it as fully as you can. What sensations do you notice in your body? Let yourself re-experience any sensations that accompanied the event, including sights, sounds, and smells. Let yourself experience the feelings you felt, the thoughts you had. How did you experience the people around you and the world around you?

Take all the time you need to relive this experience. When you have a good sense of it, see if you can name for yourself the quality (or qualities) at the heart of this experience. Is it peace, or is it joy, gratitude, clarity, wonder, acceptance, silence, caring, wholeness, or something else? What is it for you?

Take your time, and when you are ready, gently open your eyes. If you wish, take some notes.

———————

Now that your own experience of the Deep River realm is fresh in your mind, let's move on to exploring how to let more of its restorative waters flow into your everyday life.

Chapter Three

Getting Started

We cannot do everything, and there is a sense of
liberation in that. This allows us to do something,
and to do it very well. It may be incomplete,
but it is a beginning, a step along the way.
—*Bishop Ken Untener,* "Prophets of a Future
Not Our Own" ("The Romero Prayer")

This chapter begins with a word of encouragement. Although I am writing here about getting started, in fact, you have already begun the process of reclaiming your life from the tyranny of your to do's. The *recognition* that life is out of balance and the *intention* to make different choices are the critical first steps in this process. If you had not already recognized the need for more balance and resolved to do something about it, you would not be reading this book.

The suggestions in this chapter are intended to pave the way for the central practices that facilitate Deep River access, which are outlined in Part Two. As you acquaint yourself with the tools offered here and throughout the book, you will get the most value for your time and effort if you pay attention to which practices seem to resonate most with your life and what you particularly need. You don't have to do it all. Focus on and spend more time with the practices that you think will be most useful to you.

Recognize the Power of the Culture

As we saw in Chapter One, our speed-obsessed culture exerts a powerful influence on our lives, although we aren't always aware of it.

Because it is all around us, like air we breathe or like water that we swim in, we often unconsciously match our rhythms to its fast-flowing currents. To choose a slower pace, we have to become aware of the natural tendency to go along with the speeded-up rhythm that our culture encourages. Once we become conscious of cultural forces, we can begin to choose a pace and style of life that are more nurturing and balanced.

It's not hard to recognize ways in which our culture's pace and priorities have displaced, subtly or not so subtly, our own natural pace and priorities. The woman in Chapter One who had accepted call-waiting service on her telephone, along with its rhythm of unpredictable but certain interruption, is an example. When she realized that she could choose to cancel that so-called service, she was happy to take one uninterrupted phone call at a time. Greta, another woman from a Deep River group whose office was in her home, always left her computer on. When it chimed to alert her every time an e-mail arrived, she felt the need to interrupt whatever she was doing, read it, and respond right away. When she realized the toll her all-work, all-the-time rhythm was taking, Greta took a simple yet liberating step: she turned off the alert signal.

It is quite natural for our rhythms to synchronize with our environment's. Dr. Stephan Rechtshaffen calls this process "entrainment" in his book *Time Shifting*.[1] Entrainment is the tendency in nature for disparate rhythms in the physical world as well as among and between people and their environments to fall into step with one another. Rechtshaffen notes, for example, that women who live together in college dormitories often find that their menstrual cycles begin to coincide. About entraining to a rhythm in the environment, he says, "Ceremonies and religious rituals have always relied on a drumbeat or choral chant to induce a state that brings the community into a slower rhythmic frequency, enabling a more profound and spiritual experience of existence." People can be entrained to go faster, too: "We're living a rhythm that goes snap-snap-snap all the time. . . . It controls the way we walk, the way we speak, the way we respond to intimates and strangers, the way we *don't* relax. . . .

Modern society's rhythm provides perhaps the most powerful—and potentially the most pernicious—entrainment of all."[2]

It's not necessary to know the details of how entrainment works in nature to understand intuitively that when a less powerful force encounters a more powerful one, the lesser one will tend to synchronize with the greater. That's why when we as individuals encounter the force of our speed-driven culture, we hurry ourselves up to match its dominant rhythm.

When Linda, a social worker, came to one of my groups, she had been trying on and off for years to meditate. In the group, she set a goal to initiate and continue a consistent daily meditation practice. When she spoke the first night about why she signed up for the group, she said, with considerable frustration, "I *know* what I need to do, and I know it helps me. It's only fifteen or twenty minutes a day. So why is it so hard to *do* it?" My answer to Linda, and to many women who express the same frustration about their attempts to slow down, begins this way: "When you make an effort to move at a slower pace, never underestimate the power of the culture to speed you back up again."

So recognizing the power of the culture is not so much a practice to *do* but an awareness to *cultivate*. With this awareness, we are reminded that it takes effort to resist the force of the culture. It helps us to avoid the assumption that the difficulties we might encounter in the process are due to our personal failings. This awareness also supports anything else we do to downshift and slow our pace. Once we become conscious of the culture's mighty influence, we begin to see many other ways that it affects our experiences. If we can make choices about how fast we move in our daily lives, we can also make choices about how much of our time is spent marching to the culture's drumbeat of overwork, overconsumption, overactivity, interruption, distraction, and so on.

Get Support for the Deep River Process

Once we recognize the power of the culture, we can make a shift in how to think about slowing down. We move from "It shouldn't be this hard" to "Given what I'm up against, yes, it makes sense that this is not easy." Once that realization sets in, the next step is to find ways to support ourselves and our choices. The *American Heritage Dictionary* defines *support* as "to keep from weakening or failing; to strengthen." Given our tendency as individuals to synchronize with the culture, anything that strengthens our efforts to set our own pace will be helpful.

Support is the power that has energized the Deep River groups I've led for the past many years. Again and again, women find strength in what one group member calls "the sisterhood of sharing." In groups, women not only find out that others share their struggles but they also get ideas, concrete solutions to problems, new perspectives, and inspiration from each other. They give one another courage and keep one another going.

Emma, a mother of three, puts it this way: "In the safety of this circle of women, I can try out new ideas that are only half-formed. When someone here says, 'I like that; I think I'll try that,' it affirms what I've been thinking about and then allows me to go further."

Pam found support in the group for her struggle to take better care of herself. "I do a lot of giving out, and I have trouble taking in. It's an old habit that's very hard to shake. For me, it was very helpful to see women in the group focusing on themselves; it was validation for my own self-care, because these women were kindred spirits; they were not overly self-focused or overindulgent. I respected them, and so their efforts to take time for touching down into themselves reinforced my own."

Support can come in many forms. An existing community group, a book group, a church or synagogue group, or a women's group could all provide a supportive structure for working with the themes of this book. If a group is not an option, having just one other person to share with can provide needed support. And if that other person is not available, this book and other books can help you keep your momentum going. (See the Selected Reading section at the back of this book for some recommendations.) In addition to books, many other resources are available to help you slow down and find more balance in your day. For example, you might wish to explore yoga classes, relaxation tapes, workshops, lectures, or conferences. Also, broad movements such as Take Back Your Time and the Slow Food movement are gaining momentum in the United States, Canada, and Europe. Take Back Your Time is an initiative focused on empowering people and organizations to "challenge the epidemic of overwork, overscheduling, and time famine that threatens our health, our families[,] . . . our communities and our environment" (www.timeday.org). Slow Food, dedicated to "reviving the kitchen and the table as centers of pleasure, culture, and community . . . and to living a slower and more harmonious rhythm of life," began in Italy and is now active in fifty countries (www.slowfoodusa.org). More sources of support for slowing down and reclaiming your life are becoming available all the time. The key is to find the ones that work for you, and use them.

Keep a Journal

A journal is another excellent tool to help make contact with the Deep River within. I have used a journal on and off since I was ten years old. At ten, I wrote to air my grievances about family and friends and to record how I was doing in school and what my favorite TV shows were. I even named my journal and thought of it as a friend I could confide in. In my teens and early twenties, I used my journal to help me sort through the dramas of relationships and to ponder questions about the meaning of life and what *my* life might be about. As I grew into adulthood, my journal became a place to record and seek the meaning of my dreams, to work through difficulties in love and work, to give birth to creative ideas, to encourage myself when I was full of doubt or despair, and generally to listen inwardly and find myself again when I felt my life was spinning out of control.

When I was thinking about what to say about journaling in this chapter, I came across this in a journal of mine from about twelve years ago: "The value of these pages, often, is their ability to give me a space to write myself out of a funk, to write myself from 'small me' to a stepped-back larger picture, to give perspective and sometimes to touch the Deep River." Many of my entries at that time described the struggle between "small me," caught up in and overwhelmed by my to-do list, and the desire to step back, look inward, and return to myself. "What am I here for, with pen to paper? Happily anticipating a connection with myself, coming back to me—and realizing in that anticipation, how 'out' I've been, attending to others, to the garden, to getting the house in order, to the never-ending List. But the route back to myself is hard now that I've been away. Harder to find my depth, to wend my way back to the Deep River."

It was in those journal pages, where I described that small-me struggle over and over again, that the idea for my Deep River groups was born. In those pages, I explored what the group would consist of: "It will help me to name the bare bones of what I want the group to be . . . if they were to get anything from the six weeks: living silence, inner space as refuge. A course in how to nourish the soul. That has to include what you *love* to do, not just what you need to *not* do so much of."

And it was in those pages that I wrestled with my doubt and inadequacy as I planned and then encouraged myself on the eve of the first group meeting, when the perfectionist part of me tried to take over: "I can feel my energy closing in as the beginning of the group comes nearer. I lose perspective on it. Everyone I read has a program, a method, a thought-out course. . . . Well, I'm creating my course as I go. This is a pilot. . . . It doesn't need to be (and won't be!) perfect the first time. That's OK, Abby!"

There's no one way to keep a journal. The type of journaling that led to the birth of the Deep River process and that I recommend in my groups is based on Julia Cameron's "morning pages," a process described in her book *The Artist's Way.*[3] She suggests filling three pages each morning, first thing, before you eat breakfast or take a shower or brush your teeth, with literally *whatever* comes to mind. The key to this type of journaling is to let it be uncensored, stream-of-consciousness writing. As Cameron puts it, *"There is no wrong way to do morning pages"* (italics in original). With full permission to put anything and everything down on the page, from the petty to the profound, we effectively short-circuit the critical voice, or the Censor as Cameron calls it, that tends to block our creativity.

Although Cameron's focus is primarily on unblocking access to creative ideas, my experience with morning pages is that doing them also unblocks access to my deeper self. When I put all the "surface" thoughts that are going around and around in my head onto paper, (for example, "My back aches this morning; I really need to make that call to the physical therapist. . . . Oh, and I also need to call G. today. . . ."), an interesting thing happens. The tangle inside my head straightens out, quiets down, and clarity begins to appear. And if I keep writing, there is a natural movement from surface to depth. It may not happen every time I sit down to write, but it does happen some of the time, and when it does, it feels like I am being given a gift. Somehow, in the process of just writing whatever comes to mind, I drop down into a deeper place within myself, where there is always some kind of nourishment for my soul. This is the primary purpose of using a journal as a companion in the Deep River process: to create a bridge from your outer self to your inner self, to help you move from the surface of your life to the Deep River realm and receive what it has to give you.

Make a Victory Log

A victory log is another specific use of a journal that can be an important way to support yourself in the process of reclaiming your life.[4] The first step in keeping a victory log is to begin to notice your victories; then you record them in the log. A victory is any shift that you make in the direction you want to go, any step, no matter how small, toward a goal you've set for yourself. When I say "no matter how small," I really mean *no matter how small.* For example, Margaret's goal was to shift an old pattern, learned from her mother, of reacting to stress with anger. Margaret's victory occurred one afternoon when she took a deep breath and stopped herself from falling into the familiar pattern of yelling at her kids. Pat's goal was to stop pleasing others at her own expense. Her victory was to say "no" to a dinner invitation that she really wasn't interested in accepting. Kate's goal was to reduce the size of her to-do list by breaking her habit of procrastination. Kate's victory was picking up the phone and making a difficult call that she had put off for days.

Kate told me that she writes in her journal daily and faithfully records victories such as making the hard phone call. She says,

> It's during the journaling time that the victories become part of my consciousness . . . either "Oh, I was able to do this today" or "I really need to do this," and I can pep-talk myself into it. The journaling is pretty important in connection to the victories. I will often write about things that are challenging or intimidating or annoying in my life, and somehow through the writing, I can work out what the issues are that are making me procrastinate. Like calling the financial adviser: he was going to speak to me on a subject I was uncomfortable with, and I was intimidated by the fact that he was the expert and I wasn't. I was worried that I would get flustered and not get the information I needed and then feel bad after the conversation. Once I wrote about that, it naturally evolved to "If I do this, it will be a victory." I could see that the victory would be in the *making* of the phone call, and it didn't really matter how I felt when it was over. Whether I felt OK or not, whether my anxieties were reality-based or not, wasn't as important as going ahead and making the call. Categorizing the making of the call as a victory, whatever its outcome, helped me stop procrastinating. The more present the concept of "victory" is in my head, the easier it is to do the things that are hard for me to do.

Small Steps, Big Victories

One of the ways that we often keep ourselves from making progress toward greater balance in our lives is thinking that actions or choices must be significant, dramatic, revolutionary. But that's not the case at all. In working with people for nearly twenty-five years, I've found that the most effective approach to change of any kind is to think in small steps. Often, when we try to make big changes quickly, the parts of ourselves that may not be ready for drastic changes become fearful and resistant. So we become discouraged and give up when transformation doesn't happen immediately. Of course, there are instances when we do make big shifts, either because we choose to take a needed leap or because life presents us with one. But more often, change happens in a less dramatic fashion. Working toward goals in small, manageable steps is less likely to elicit resistance, so that we can ease into new patterns. When we count each small step achieved as a victory, we give ourselves encouragement, which is fuel to keep going.

When Elsa came to do therapy with me, she was a "leaper." She had a vivid imagination that yielded many creative ideas and not much patience for carrying them out. Part of her reason for beginning therapy was that her leaping had cost her; Elsa was looking for ways to slow down and consider her choices more carefully. The leap that had wreaked havoc on her life was a precipitous decision to move from the East Coast to California: "I was overwhelmed with work, working seven days a week. There was so much pressure to keep going that there was no relief, no balance. So my remedy for that was to move to a new city! Where I knew no one! And by the way, I was four months pregnant! That was a typical leap for me." Elsa and her husband had given little time or energy to market research before moving. As soon as they made the move, the one possible work prospect fell through. Elsa quickly learned that there was a recession in California and that all the work in her field was back east. Neither she nor her husband could get a job, and, as she described it, "the bottom fell out from under us."

They eventually moved back east and began to pick up the pieces. Looking back now, Elsa sees the move to California as a pivotal experience that turned her toward a new way of making changes in her life. Once she was settled in a new job, we began to practice taking small steps toward manageable goals. For years, Elsa had wanted to get back to the painting she had done earlier in her life but felt she couldn't because of lack of time, space, and support, all fueled by self-doubt about her ability as an artist. We broke the seemingly impossible goal of getting back to painting into small steps. First, she had to ask for support from her husband. Asking was hard for her to do, but the support from him came easily once she told him what she needed. Then she had to carve out a space in her home to paint. The basement was the only option at the time; another step was getting a dumpster, then cleaning out the basement. Once the space was set up, she had to carve out time: "I had to take back a day a week; that was difficult, not because my work hours were inflexible, but because of the guilt. It was so monumental at first. It was like climbing Mt. Everest to take Fridays off. But once I started doing it, it became easier. And now, of course! Fridays are my day." The next step was to actually do it, to sit down and paint. The small steps had served her so well that even when she felt self-doubt, it did not have the power to stop her. Step by step, Elsa restructured her life to include a form of creative expression that gives her a sense of well-being and great satisfaction. "When I'm doing the art, it's like I've arrived, and I'm at peace with the world."

A note here before I continue with Elsa's story: if, as you were reading, you found yourself thinking, "I could *never* take a whole day off" or any thought along the lines of "Maybe *she* could do that, but that would never work for me," make a mental note of that thought. The section on blocking beliefs later in the chapter will address thoughts like these. It's true that Elsa had unusual job flexibility and that many of us wouldn't be able to take a whole day off each week. But we all *can* find small steps toward our goals that are workable for us.

As Elsa continued to practice achieving goals in small steps, a new, more measured approach to change began to replace her habit of leaping. Recently, she went for the first time with her family to visit a beloved place where she had lived for several years as a child.

I came back with the idea "Wouldn't it be great to move there?" The new behavior was that I didn't pack up my bags and move. It's a year and several months later, and we're still talking about it, but we're doing little steps; we're exploring it, testing things, carefully analyzing everything. We're asking ourselves, "What will it really look like, and is that what we want?" It's taking time and energy, yes, but honestly, it's more fun. And though I can see it in my mind as a fait accompli, it doesn't mean that this is the right time for it, and I'm OK with that. The difference between that and what I used to do is like night and day.

For Elsa, learning how to take small steps has yielded some big victories: she has been able to bring painting, a creative activity that brings her great joy, back into her life, and she is able to deliberate maturely rather than act impulsively about important life decisions. In fact, all of our victories, no matter how small, are big in two ways: first, any action or new way of thinking that breaks the inertia of habit has the potential to foster a turn in a desired direction. Second, victories achieved can build on one another and, over time, create a reservoir of success, as well as additional momentum for change.

Blocking Beliefs

My first act of free will shall be to believe in free will.
—*William James*[5]

At this point, I've given enough suggestions for slowing down and reclaiming your life that if you weren't already thinking somewhere in the back of your mind, "I don't have *time* for this!" you may well be thinking it now. Such a thought is an example of a blocking belief.[6] Blocking beliefs are the thoughts, sometimes conscious, sometimes not, that stop us before we get started. They're the mental naysayers that hinder our momentum in making changes. We usually try to deal with these beliefs by ignoring them. We do our best to keep them on the periphery or totally out of our awareness. The problem with this approach is, simply, that it doesn't work.

Let's say that I know I want to read this book and begin to act on some of the suggestions in order to rebalance my life. As I read, the thought "I don't have *time* for this!" begins to creep into the back of my mind, so I shoo it away and go back to reading. What I may notice next is that I get very sleepy or that I remember something on my list that just *has* to be done right now. Or I may finish reading the chapter but decide I don't need to do any of the exercises. Or I may do the exercises, but the next time I sit down to read, I somehow have lost the book. Sound familiar? One way or another, "I don't have time for this," if it isn't examined consciously, can effectively derail my intention.

Once an underlying belief becomes conscious, I can make a choice about it. If I'm not aware that I am holding a particular belief, my behavior will be limited by that mind-set or assumption. In fact, this is a fundamental psychological principle that underlies much of the work described in this book. When we become conscious of forces that affect us unconsciously, we are then empowered to make choices about our actions.

In this section and in the next six chapters, I will name some of the most common beliefs that get in the way of individual progress and offer some strategies for working with these mind-sets in order to neutralize their negative effects. In working with any belief, it is important to understand that a belief is not the same as the truth. This may seem obvious, but when we operate from unexamined beliefs, we are acting as if they are the truth.

Blocking Belief: "I don't have time for this!"

Let's look more carefully at "I don't have time for this," one of the most common assumptions in our fast-forward, time-starved culture.

Sara is a client of mine who is a college student. She had been doing well for quite some time, until she and her boyfriend broke up, which prompted her to call me. She was feeling depressed and insecure, and an old fear of spending time alone had resurfaced. Previously, when we had worked on her fear of being by herself, Sara had reconnected with a very positive experience from high school when she had gone on a wilderness trip that included a solo segment. During her time alone, Sara had done a lot of journaling and had come away with a great sense of confidence and wholeness. She had used journaling on and off since then as a way to reconnect with her inner strength. So I suggested that she get out her journal and do some writing a few times a week. Sara's first response was, "I just don't have time for that. I've got so much work for my classes right now, and soccer takes a huge chunk of time, and I'm volunteering at the local shelter and don't want to give that up." We went back and forth a bit about her schedule and where she might squeeze in some journaling time, but nothing seemed to be right. It was true that she had a lot on her plate, but finally, I pointed out that she had managed to find time for this hour with me. "How did you do that?" I asked. "Oh!" she said, "You're right. Good point. Yes, I did make this time. Oh, yeah." In that moment, Sara broke through the "I don't have time for this" belief. Until then, she had truly felt that she objectively did not have the time. After Sara came to the realization that it was possible to find time in her schedule, we were able to come up with three times during the next week when she could write in her journal.

This example illustrates the power of an underlying belief. It *feels* as if it is objectively true. There certainly are situations in which it *is* true that we don't have time for something. But an underlying assumption that we don't have time, usually held in place by unconscious feelings, prevents us from even thinking about how we *might* create time for what we want to do. Sometimes, as in Sara's case, all we need is a challenge to the assumption we're making so that we can see through it and move beyond it. At other times, blocking beliefs are more deeply rooted and we need to take a look at their origins in order to free ourselves from their power. These types of beliefs will be covered in later chapters.

If "I don't have time for this" is a blocking belief you've identified in yourself, take a few moments now to do the exercise that follows. If lack of time is not coming up for you as you read, check to see if there are any other beliefs that might be blocking you at this point in the process. If you made a mental note of a negative thought as you were reading Elsa's story, that might be your blocking belief. Some other examples might be "Other people can do this kind of thing, but I'm no good at it" or "If I really slow down, I'll be too out of sync with my friends [my spouse, my family, my coworkers]." If you identify a blocking belief, write it down, then do steps 2 through 4 of the exercise.

Important note: There might *not* be anything blocking you right now. Don't assume that there is a blocking belief every step of the way. If you don't sense any significant emotional or mental drag on your motivation to move forward with the process, just keep going!

⁂ Exercise: Moving Beyond "I Don't Have Time for This"

This exercise is an opportunity to disempower the belief that you have no time to slow down and regain control of your life.

1. Make a list of all the reasons that you can't possibly spend time reading this book and doing the exercises. Getting this list of what's in the way out of your head and onto paper will be helpful in itself. You might list reasons like these:

   - My job is too demanding.
   - I read too slowly.
   - I'm too tired at night, and that's the only time I have to read.
   - This kind of thing never works for me anyway; I shouldn't waste time on it.
   - I have young kids at home; I don't have enough free time.

   Write down anything and everything that has to do with why you can't.

2. After you have listed all the reasons why you can't do it, ask yourself, "What is my motivation for reading this book and doing the exercises?" (It's easy to lose sight of why we *want* to do something when we get buried under the barrage of why we can't.) Be specific, and write it down. For example, you might list reasons such as the following:

- I want to feel less stress and more calm in my daily routine.
- I want to feel free and willing to focus on my kids when they're home from school.
- I want to have some time every day when I recharge my own batteries, whatever that takes.
- I want to include guilt-free relaxation and play as well as work and obligation in my week.
- I want to make time for my drawing [singing, sewing, sculpting, or whatever your creative interest is] now, not ten years from now.

3. Now ask yourself, "What belief would *reinforce* rather than block my intention to read this book?" For example, you might tell yourself,

- I can choose to make time for the most important things in my life. Or,
- My watch doesn't control my life; I do.

Write down your new belief. Say it to yourself a few times. It's OK if you don't believe it fully; say it anyway.

4. When you sit down to read or do one of the exercises, try beginning by repeating your new belief to yourself. It may seem artificial or contrived at first. Do it anyway. Whenever "I don't have time for this" shows up in your thoughts, try consciously substituting your new belief, and see what the effect is.

⚘ Exercise: Start a Journal, Record a Victory

Should you choose to keep a journal, what's most important is that it be workable for you in *your* life. If that means doing "morning pages" in the evening, great. If it means journaling three (or fewer) times a week during lunch hour or just on weekends, that's fine. Most people write with a pen on paper; a woman in one of my groups had fibromyalgia that made the physical act of writing hard for her, so she wrote her journal on her computer. If that works better for you, do it.

Before you begin, give some thought to where and when you will write in your journal. This is important for two reasons: it is more likely to happen if it fits well with *your* life and your daily rhythm, and it is more likely to happen if you don't leave it to chance.

Some women are concerned about privacy. "What if someone finds my journal and reads it?" they ask. If you think using a journal will be a source of support, please don't let this worry stop you. Sometimes, when examined, this fear turns out to be a blocking belief, a fear with no real substance. If there is a valid concern, there are ways to ensure enough privacy. Some women that I've worked with have come up with secure hiding places. Some women write and then tear up the pages. While it can be useful to look back at what you have written from time to time, the *process* of writing is more important than the product. It is better to write and destroy the writing than not to write at all.

If you do not already have a journal, find a blank book that works for you. I have used everything from beautiful cloth-covered journals to artist's sketchbooks to inexpensive spiral-bound notebooks from the drugstore. If fancy and beautiful brings out your critic ("A beautiful book should have beautiful writing"), visit the drugstore. If cheap and simple is uninviting, find a blank book that makes you smile and invites you to open it when you look at the cover.

Most important of all, begin! If you have used a journal before, use this Deep River process as motivation to start again or to keep going. If you have never used a journal, this is an opportunity to try it and see for yourself what value it has for you. Give it at least two weeks; after that, you can decide if you want to keep going.

Once you begin your journal, record at least one victory in the first week. Again, a victory is any step, no matter how small, in the direction of a goal you've set for yourself. Getting yourself a journal is a victory. Setting up a journaling schedule is a victory. Writing in it one day is a victory. That's three already!

Even if you don't use a journal for anything else, I recommend keeping a victory log. You can make it a separate section of your journal or a separate part of any journal page, or you can simply include a record of your victories as you write. You can use a highlighter or star them in a different color to help them stand out. To help you get started, you will find some victory log pages at the end of this book. If you don't want to keep a journal, you can keep a record of your victories right there. Recording victories by writing them down helps to fix them in your awareness as positive reference points. In times of doubt or discouragement, it's helpful to be able to see your victories on the page and remember the progress you have already made.

———————

The preliminary practices described in this chapter—recognizing the power of the culture, getting support, and keeping a journal—are helpful tools for bringing more balance and depth into everyday life. In addition, they prepare the ground for the practices outlined in Part Two, which form the core of the Deep River process.

Part Two

Touching the Deep River

The Practices

The next six chapters flesh out the essential tools for freeing ourselves from the tyranny of our to-do lists and allowing nourishment from the Deep River to flow into our daily lives. At times, the rich waters of the Deep River realm may bubble up unbidden into life at the surface. If we see sunlight fall a certain way on a snow-covered tree or we happen to pause long enough to look into the eyes of a child, we might spontaneously slow down, open up, and touch the Deep River. It sometimes happens, we might say, through grace. We cannot *make* it happen. But what we *can* do is *create conditions in our daily lives that invite more access to the Deep River realm*. The tools in the next six chapters, along with the suggestions outlined in Chapter Three, are the means toward this end. Again, you don't have to do every one. It's helpful to think in small steps and to be selective, focusing on the practices that address what is most needed in your own life. All together, you will find in these chapters a substantial toolbox for finding balance and depth in everyday life.

Chapter Four

Take Time-In

Certain springs are tapped only when we are alone.
—*Anne Morrow Lindbergh*, Gift from the Sea

In Anne Morrow Lindbergh's classic book of essays, *Gift from the Sea*, she shares her reflections on women in relationship and solitude. Written more than fifty years ago, this lovely book contains wisdom that is still timely for women. She says, "Women need solitude in order to find again the true essence of themselves: that firm strand which will be the indispensable center of a whole web of human relationships."[1] In this passage and elsewhere, she is pointing to what I consider the most fundamental practice in the Deep River process: taking time-in. "Time-in" is a little like what we mean when we use the expression "time-out." With children, time-outs are usually given in a stressful or out-of-control situation as an opportunity for the child (and often the adult) to calm down. In sports, coaches use allotted time-outs to help the team step back from the action, rethink strategy, rest and reorient themselves, and slow down the game. Both time-out and time-in describe taking a break from what we are doing, but when we take a time-out, we usually step away from some activity just long enough to get back to it. Time-*in* emphasizes not the activity we're getting away from, but the *quality* of the time spent away. When we take time-in, we step away from outer demands and responsibilities, cut down on distraction, and gather ourselves inward. One characteristic is essential to this practice: time-in is time spent alone.

The purpose of time-in is to find the firm strand that Lindbergh speaks of. We need to pull away from the roles, relationships, and activities that ordinarily define us and enter into solitude in order to find our true essence and come more directly into relationship with ourselves rather than defining ourselves primarily through our roles as partners, spouses, coworkers, mothers, sisters, friends, and so on.

How to Take Time-In

There are myriad ways to take time-in. For Carla, a mother of two young children, time-in is sitting at the kitchen table and drinking a cup of tea during their naptime. For Judy, time-in is a lunch-hour walk in the woods near her office building. For Kay, time-in is journaling first thing in the morning.

Tara has turned her morning commute into her time-in. She knows the route well, and most of it is highway driving. She calls it her "in-between time"; in between the demands of home and work, she chooses to leave the radio and the cell phone off and just be in silence as she drives. "It's not the deep silence of the back woods," she says, "but it *is* quiet relative to both home and work most of the time. And no one interrupts me! I can think my own thoughts in peace."

Catherine's time-in is her morning run. "When I'm running, all the list making clears out of my head. I'm just there, with my breathing, with my body moving, with the air, the pavement. It brings me back to basics, back to myself."

Time-in can be sitting in a chair looking out a window, doing nothing; it can be meditating or praying or journaling or listening to music or drawing. It might be taking a walk, but it *isn't* taking a power walk while listening to a radio and using a stopwatch to time yourself, making sure you go fast enough to keep your heart rate up. It is also not taking a walk with a friend, as lovely as that can be. The key characteristics of time-in, whatever form it takes, are as follows:

- It is time without interruption, distraction, or multitasking.
- It is time spent by yourself, with yourself.
- While you might be doing an activity, the emphasis is on *being* with yourself more than on *doing* the activity.

Not every activity is conducive to taking time-in. When I first described time-in to one of my groups, one woman said, "Usually when I have a little time to myself, I go to the mall to get a couple of errands done. I guess that's not what you're talking about, is it?" No, that's not what I'm talking about.

Madeleine L'Engle, in her autobiographical book *A Circle of Quiet*, gives a good example of what I *am* talking about:

> Every so often I need OUT. . . . I have to get away from everybody—away from all these people I love most in the world—in order to regain a sense of proportion. . . . Often I need to get away completely, if only for a few minutes. My special place is a small brook in a green glade, a circle of quiet from which there is no visible sign of human beings. There's a natural stone bridge over the brook, and I sit there, dangling my legs and looking through the foliage at the sky reflected in the water, and things slowly come back into perspective. . . . If I sit for a while, then my impatience, crossness, frustration, are indeed annihilated, and my sense of humor returns.[2]

The purpose and effect of time-in is the deep renewal that comes from gathering oneself inward and being in solitude. Time-in is a doorway to the Deep River realm. Renewal through solitary retreat is a time-honored practice in most of the world's major religions. Christianity, Judaism, Islam, Buddhism, and Hinduism all include traditions of spiritual retreat as part of their wisdom teachings. Since most of us can't easily leave our life for extended periods of retreat time, time-in is a way to incorporate solitude into our life just as it is, on a daily basis, so that we can receive regular nourishment from the Deep River realm.

Traditionally, time for turning inward also occurs on a weekly basis in the form of a Sabbath day. The Sabbath in the Judeo-Christian and Muslim traditions is intended to be sacred time, a time to slow down, rest, reflect, and turn away from material concerns toward the life of the spirit. It is a time of being rather than doing.

When my children were very young, I remember the feeling L'Engle describes of needing to "get away completely." The need for solitude eventually led me to create what I called my "sanctuary days." I worked out a schedule with my husband so that once a month on Sunday, I would leave the house for several hours. It was never a whole day; usually, it was just three or four hours. Sometimes I would actually go to a nearby monastery that accepted guests, or in warmer weather, I would walk in the woods. Sometimes I would sit by myself in a café or restaurant where I could be anonymous and write in my journal. I purposely left my home so that I could be away not only from my family but also from the pull of the ever-present to do's of the house.

This more extended time-in once a month was a lifeline for me, helping me keep my balance in the years when child rearing was the most demanding. When my children were older, I began to take weeklong silent retreats once a year. Once you understand the importance of time-in and experience its benefits, you can look for ways to incorporate it into your life on a daily, weekly, monthly, or yearly basis—or all of the above!

Obstacles to Taking Time-In

If taking time-in is such a simple practice, why do so many of us find it difficult to do? One answer is that this kind of time is not valued in our culture, nor do we ourselves always appreciate its importance. Anne Morrow Lindbergh's observations about alone-time in our culture are just as relevant now as they were half a century ago:

> The world today does not understand, in either man or woman, the need to be alone. How inexplicable it seems. Anything else will be accepted as a better excuse. If one sets aside time for a business appointment, a trip to the hairdresser, a social engagement, or a shopping expedition, that time is accepted as inviolable. But if one says: I cannot come because that is my hour to be alone, one is considered rude, egotistical or strange. What a commentary on our civilization, when being alone is considered suspect; when one has to apologize for it, make excuses, hide the fact that one practices it—like a secret vice![3]

Time spent alone may also be devalued by the common perception in this culture that women are better off being with someone than being alone. Women tend to be defined *in relationship*. We learn that we should not spend time alone by choice, but only if an other isn't available to be with. Being alone is assumed to be the same as being lonely. If loneliness has been our primary experience when we are by ourselves, it is not surprising that we would associate one with the other. Unless we can separate loneliness from being alone, we won't put a high priority on seeking the solitude of time-in. Writer and poet May Sarton says, "Loneliness is the poverty of self. Solitude is the richness of self."[4] Knowing the difference between the two makes time-in much more inviting. (For more on knowing the difference, see the "Blocking Belief" section at the end of this chapter.)

Because we do not live in a culture that values contemplation and reflection, and solitude is not a societal norm, it may be difficult to take time-in simply because we do not really know how to do it. When Marilyn, a mother of three and a full-time marketing executive, began to participate in a Deep River group, the concept of time-in was utterly foreign to her. She prided herself on being able to juggle the responsibilities of her career and home life in addition to several volunteer projects in her community, usually without missing a beat. The thought of being by herself and "doing nothing," even for a short period of time, made her extremely uncomfortable. While I've encountered many women who have had some experience with intentional solitude, others, like Marilyn, need to begin by simply considering the possibility of time-in and what it might have to offer. They need a chance to rethink their assumption that being outwardly focused and keeping busy is always the best choice. When Marilyn decided to try taking time-in, she began by sitting still on a chair in her living room by herself for just five minutes, which seemed like an eternity at first. Approaching her alone times in small steps, she worked gradually up to sitting for ten minutes by herself. At first, her time-in was filled with thoughts about wasting time and what else she could be getting done or *would* be getting done as soon as she got up. But eventually, Marilyn got more comfortable with this time of just being, without doing, and began to look forward to it as a chance to pause, take stock of how she was feeling, and take a break from the constant motion of getting things checked off her list. She didn't do it every day, but she began to be able to sense when she just needed to sit still.

There are two other reasons that the seemingly straightforward practice of taking time-in is not so easy to do. The first is simply that our outer lives intrude on us. If we don't claim this kind of time for ourselves, most likely it will not happen. Too many other things—our to-do list, our job, our home, our possessions, our relationships, our community—clamor for our time and attention. Because the multiple demands we face daily are a formidable force, we need to learn how to make clear boundaries. This is such an important skill, not only for taking time-in but for living a life of depth and meaning, that it gets its own chapter as one of the Deep River practices.

The final reason that taking time-in can be hard to do is that when we cut down on distraction and spend time alone, feelings, thoughts, and life issues that we have pushed to the periphery of our awareness may emerge, and that can be scary. Getting comfortable with difficult feelings facilitates taking time-in and lowers the resistance we might have to any kind of deep contact with ourselves. So befriending feelings is another Deep River practice; I address it in Chapter Six.

The Gifts of Time-In

Time-in brings us benefits that are immeasurable and that we won't easily get otherwise. Educator Parker Palmer says, "We were made for solitude. Our lives may be rich in relationships, but the human self remains a mystery of enfolded inwardness that no other person can possibly enter and know. If we fail to embrace our ultimate aloneness and seek meaning only in communion with others, we wither and die. . . . The farther we travel toward the great Mystery, the more at home we must be with our essential aloneness in order to stay healthy and whole."[5]

Since the power of our achievement-driven, doing-oriented culture works against taking time-in, I think that readers could use some encouragement to begin or revitalize this practice, so I am providing some examples of women who have successfully learned to incorporate it into their lives. I hope that hearing what this simple practice brings to them will inspire you to make time-in a regular practice in your life.

Angela: "My walk is time with Spirit."

Angela's time-in is an early morning walk in the woods near her home. She says, "It's as if, when I walk into the woods, there's a threshold I step over that says, 'and now you can leave the rest behind.' My walk is time with Spirit; it's almost like a prayer." She has been doing this "walking prayer in nature" for nine years now. Angela is a small woman with a delicate frame, but she will walk no matter what the weather—ice, sleet, snow, wind, rain, extreme heat or cold—through the full range of New England's varied seasons. Her steadiness with this practice both feeds and is fed by the benefits she feels. "There's something very powerful about walking the same land every day through all the seasons. I've never done a practice in the same place for such a long time. It's such an anchor for me. If I don't walk, I feel like a caged animal. I start to feel like I'm boxed in by the culture we live in, which says, 'It has to be This Way,' and each thing it says is a bar of the cage."

Her walks not only give Angela a sense of freedom but also prepare her for what she needs to do each day. Over time, this practice has given her a greater capacity to handle her life:

> I can juggle more balls but also be more present than I would have been if I didn't walk. The daily walking has allowed the container I hold my life in to expand. Say you start with a small container as a child, and each year it grows with the experience, the knowledge, the wisdom you gather. Somehow, the walking has allowed the container

to grow beyond where I imagined it could. So my "container" now has more space, and I can do more, handle more. I'm able to be the mother, the daughter, the friend, the partner, the professional.

Also, prior to the practice of walking, I was much more rigid about things. I had to have order, I couldn't handle chaos. The walking has allowed me to tolerate—and actually seek, in some cases— what isn't organized, what isn't laid out in a linear way. Before, I was so focused on the next thing on the list, the next task, holding on to everything and feeling very rigid about it.

For Angela, the effects of her daily morning practice have permeated her life in a gradual way. About letting go of rigidity, she says, "Slowly, not even consciously, the shift over time took me to this more spacious way of thinking and being. I even look back at pictures of myself and I can see the difference between before I started walking and now." Angela also gradually found that she was able to receive the benefit of walking even when she couldn't get to the woods:

> When I first went back to a corporate job, I couldn't quite get the rhythm of getting up *that* early to walk and then make the train. But I noticed on the train that I could close my eyes and be in the woods. I could be in this place that I had walked for such a long time. That astounded me! I could just be with what I know my feet sound like on the earth, with the water, the trees. . . . I realized then that I had incorporated what the earth has shared with me into my tapestry, into my own personal being. That took years, and I didn't even know it was happening!

Dorothy: "It's an issue of happiness."

Dorothy's time-in is always in the late afternoon, although how she spends the time varies. Sometimes, it's journaling; more often, it's about thirty minutes of meditation, usually outdoors. She says simply, "It's an issue of happiness. If I don't take that time, I don't feel as happy. If I don't gather my thoughts in some way toward the end of the day, either articulating them by journaling or letting them settle by meditating, then I'm either irritated at other people or I'm unsure of myself, or both." Dorothy began to create intentional solitude in her afternoons about seven years ago. As her time-in became a more consistent part of her daily routine, Dorothy noticed a subtle effect it was having:

> When I begin my time-in, I'm often kind of tight, and my focus is narrow. It *literally* is narrow at first. Usually, I'm only aware of what I'm sitting right in front of. By the end of the time, I'm more aware of things at the periphery of my visual field. It seems to actually expand my vision. It isn't something I'm planning to do; it just happens. And I think that's a metaphor for what happens in my thinking. I might be focused on some problem I've been wrestling with all afternoon, and that's all I can see in my mind when I start sitting. As I meditate or write, the outside world comes in a little more or I see the problem more in perspective. I feel settled in myself, and I have an idea of what I can do to open things up.

Dorothy describes having what she calls "a broader field," in which more creative possibilities come to her about how to deal with or respond to many different life situations. "I let more ideas come in about how to handle a delicate interaction between people I supervise at work or between family members. Or I let things expand from the first idea I have about how to sew something, and I come up with new ideas about how to make a shirt or a dress."

This kind of shift to a "broader field" as a result of taking time-in is subtle and a little hard to describe, yet for Dorothy it is priceless and well worth the time she takes at the end of her afternoon. It not only affects the quality of her relationships and her creative work; it is a key to her overall sense of happiness with her life.

Lydia: "There's a certain way that I have relaxed into life."

Lydia is a social worker with a satisfying but extremely demanding job as director of a social service agency. Her children are grown now, but one of them has a chronic illness that is an ongoing source of concern. When she called me, Lydia told me that just reading the description of the Deep River group had brought her to tears. While the concepts were not new to her, she realized that she could use help to incorporate the Deep River practices more fully and consistently in her life. Lydia already had a way of taking time-in. The group helped her to add some new elements to it and commit to it more wholeheartedly. Here is what she does:

> I've created a little ritual in the morning. I get up at 5:30. I make a cup of tea, cover it, and put it in what was once my daughter's bedroom, where I have a little writing table. Then I go into what was my son's room, and I meditate for twenty minutes. Doing the meditation consistently is new, and it's very hard for me; my mind is constantly warbling away at me, even at that hour, but I do it because it helps me. Then I go across the hall to what was my daughter's room; I have four candles there, and I light them all. I write a little in my journal. When I'm done, I speak to the candles. One of them is for my husband, and one each for my two kids, and one is for me. There used to just be three on the table, for the three of them, but since taking the group I have added one: for me. My children are adults now, but there are certain things I want to keep saying to them, so I say them every morning. And then I say something to myself, like, "You can trust more" or "Open yourself more"—something along those lines.
>
> Then I blow the candles out, and if I have time, I go for a walk with the dog. There's a field near where I live—there's something about that field—I just feel like I need to stop there and feel grateful. I say a prayer of gratitude (while my dog is racing around!), and then I'll come home and start my day.

Do you think, as you read about Lydia's morning time-in, "I could *never* take that much time for myself at the beginning of the day—or *any* time of day!"? Lydia has had those kind of thoughts herself, but this is what she says now:

I have a two-hour routine in the morning. I have to be out of the house by 7:30. I thought at first that taking this time was sort of a selfish thing. I also used to feel like somehow it was weak to need this. I should just charge out of bed and get back out on the battle-field! Now I've decided that it takes two hours every morning for me to gather the strength that I really need. I have big things to deal with, so it's going to take two hours every day. If that's what it takes, then that's what it takes.

The time-invested in her morning ritual has paid off for Lydia. She describes the impact like this:

It has really helped me reduce the sense of anxiety and pressure that I put on myself. There's a certain way that I have relaxed into life. Recently, I had the ultimate test of doing something differently— my in-laws came for their yearly visit. It's always a challenge, but this year I glided through it. I didn't have the normal anticipatory anxiety; I was able to talk to them in a kind and caring way, which has been hard for me in the past; and I actually felt grateful to them for what they've done for me and the kids all these years. My attitude was very different. My better approach affected my husband's ability to cope well with the visit, so he also got through the week with minimal stress.

Another benefit that is surprising to Lydia is her physical energy. In order to add meditation to her ritual, she set the alarm a half hour earlier, at 5:30 A.M. rather than 6. "But," she says, with a tone of surprise, "I'm not tired. I get six hours of sleep a night, and I'm fine. No need for that afternoon Snickers bar. I'm fine!"

While having physical stamina is very valuable to Lydia, even more important, she feels, is having access to a deep sense of inner strength. This is the core quality of contacting the Deep River within for her. She says, "I've always had the reputation of being someone who is extraordinarily calm, who handles stress and crisis well. But when my boss, for example, has told me that, I've always thought, 'You should see what it feels like on the inside. You should go a little bit below skin deep. It does *not* look like that inside!' But now, I feel like it kind of *does* look like that inside. It kind of does."

For many women, making time for just one element that Lydia incorporates in her morning ritual—meditation *or* journaling *or* walking in nature—would be a victory and perhaps all that would be needed. Whether you take twenty minutes or two hours is not important. What's important is to ask yourself the question, "What will it take for me to replenish myself?" and to listen for the answer.

Angela, Dorothy, and Lydia have well-established practices of taking time-in. While some benefits of this practice need time to gradually ripen and bear fruit, others are immediately apparent. You don't need to take time-in for years before it begins to bring balance and depth into your life. Start where you are, take small steps, and keep going. You will notice the difference it makes in your daily routine, in your relationships, and in your ability to touch the Deep River.

Blocking Belief:
"If I'm alone, I'll be empty and lonely."

To truly embed the practice of taking time-in in our lives as Angela, Dorothy, and Lydia have done, we may first need to address the blocking belief that associates aloneness with loneliness. The power of beliefs such as this one is that they are partly true. For most of us, being alone includes the experience of loneliness at least some of the time. But as we saw earlier in this chapter, being alone and being lonely are not necessarily one and the same. If you tend to stay away from time alone and you recognize this blocking belief as part of the reason, I invite you to consider the following ways to address and challenge your assumption:

• *Take a look at the roots of this belief in your experience.* What life experiences have contributed to your tendency to equate time spent alone with loneliness? Use your journal or a pen and paper to write down any memories of loneliness that come to mind. The memories could be from childhood, from more recently, or both. They might be your own experience or what you witnessed as you were growing up about how significant people in your life dealt with loneliness. In addition to memories of loneliness, do you have memories of being *perceived* negatively by others (for example, with pity or scorn) when alone? These experiences can contribute to feeling lonely rather than simply alone.

You can record the memories in brief or write about them more extensively. The purpose is simply to become conscious of what experiences may have given rise to feeling lonely when alone.

• *Create a reservoir of positive associations with being alone.* Take a fresh sheet of paper, or begin a new journal entry, and write down any positive experiences of being alone that you can remember. Have you ever felt happy or contented while reading, walking, listening to music, gardening, taking a shower—or doing *anything*—alone? Write down any memories you have of feeling good while alone. The memories could be of brief moments or longer stretches of time. They could be memories from childhood or from more recently in your life, or both. Record the memories in brief or write about them more extensively—whatever feels right to you. Remembering and writing down these experiences is itself a way of challenging the assumption that being alone always means being lonely.

• *Create a new belief that reflects your positive associations with being alone.* Here is an example of a positive mind-set about alone time from May Sarton: "I am happy to be alone—time to think, time to be. This kind of open-ended time is the only luxury that really counts and I feel stupendously rich to have it."[6] You can borrow from Sarton or anyone else whose attitude toward solitude you find appealing or admirable, or you can create your own new belief. Some examples:

"I like spending time alone."

"I am happy by myself."

"I can feel whole and fulfilled by myself."

"Time alone gives me a chance to make better friends with myself."

"I am open to what solitude has to teach me."

Write down your new belief, and say it to yourself a few times. It's OK if you don't believe it fully. Say it anyway.

Remember that having a new belief to work with doesn't mean you should never be lonely. We all experience loneliness sometimes. Your new belief, however, is a reminder that solitude can also bring joy, contentment, depth, and richness.

• *Practice intentional solitude, using the principle of small steps.* Set aside a small amount of time-in. Start with a doable amount, no matter how small, and add time in small increments. As you begin your time-in, repeat your new belief to yourself. It may seem artificial or contrived at first. Do it anyway, and see what the effect is. When you have a positive experience of spending time alone, write it down as a victory, adding to your reservoir of positive associations with being alone.

Exercise: Making Time to Take Time-In

The best way to ensure that time-in will become part of your daily routine is to plan for it. This exercise is a tool for planning. By giving a little thought to when, where, and how you will take time-in, you are setting your intention and supporting your efforts to incorporate this renewing practice into your life. Two of the three women whose time-in I described earlier in the chapter begin their day with intentional solitude. Many women find this works well because gathering themselves inward in the morning helps to set the tone for the entire day. However, morning is not necessarily the best time for everyone. Listen to yourself, and experiment with different times if you need to. It's important that you take time-in when it works for *you*.

1. Begin by asking yourself, "What already works?" If you have some form of time-in practice that works for you, great! Or

perhaps there is something you already do that you've never thought of as time-in. One group member realized that watering and tending her plants in the nighttime quiet after everyone else went to bed was a way of getting back in touch with herself; this became her time-in.

If you identify something that already works, then ask, "Can I do it more often, more regularly, for longer, or just give myself full permission to do it?" This is an opportunity to identify and revitalize the time-in that's already part of your life. Then go to step 4.

2. If your current life doesn't include time-in, brainstorm on paper about a few possible ways to try it. For example,

   • Write in your journal for twenty minutes before work.
   • Stop, breathe, sit still for ten minutes before the kids come home.
   • Listen to relaxing music or a relaxation tape before bed.
   • Take that meditation or yoga class, and try practicing at home.
   • Take a lunchtime walk alone.
   • Close the door to your office and look out the window for five minutes.

3. Choose one of your ideas to try out. Once again, the key here is to think in small steps. Choose something doable and possible with only small adjustments to your life as it is. If the thought of meditation seems like climbing a steep mountain after not exercising for years, don't choose it! If the thought of taking twenty minutes makes you immediately edgy, start with five or ten. Once you have some victories with taking time-in, you can adjust and expand what you do if you choose to.

4. Look at your calendar or think about your daily routine, and plan when, where, and how you will take time-in. Then take the following steps:

   • Write down your plan in the present tense, as if you have already incorporated it into your life. Be as specific as you can—for example, "On Mondays, Wednesdays, and Fridays, I sit in the kitchen at 4 P.M. and have a cup of tea by myself."

- Write down any obstacles, inner or outer, that might get in your way. An inner obstacle might be the blocking belief discussed in this chapter, the one that associates being alone with loneliness. An outer obstacle might be lack of quiet time or quiet space before work because your children are awake and need to get out the door then.

- Think about and write down ideas on what you can do about any obstacles you have named. Working with inner obstacles usually involves a shift of mental attitude about time-in. The preceding "Blocking Belief" section suggests some ways to make a mental shift away from associating alone time with loneliness. If your inner obstacle is the fear that you won't get enough done if you take time-in, here are some ways to encourage a shift of attitude:
  - Start with a very small increment of time, such as five minutes.
  - Make an agreement with your to-do list that if it leaves you alone for time-in, you will attend to it for two hours after that.
  - Find a buddy to help you remember that five or ten minutes of sitting still probably won't result in catastrophe.
  - Begin your time-in with a little reading from this book or another book that can remind you about why this kind of time is important, even if something else doesn't get done until later.
  - Make an agreement with yourself to try it for one week, then see if you want to continue or change your plan.

Working with outer obstacles usually involves some creative scheduling. If your kids are up and about too early for you to have morning quiet time, maybe your time-in will need to be in the afternoon or the evening or on the weekend. If you don't have a room of your own at home, maybe your time-in will need to take place in a quiet room at the library while your kids attend children's reading hour. You can be as creative as you want in getting around obstacles. If your obstacles have to do with the demands of your life impinging on your time-in, you might want to read Chapter Five on making boundaries and do the exercises at the end of it.

- Try out your plan! Give it at least a week, then adjust it as needed. Write down your victories, and share them with a friend or a Deep River buddy.

In order to take time-in, we need to choose it. I take comfort in knowing that while life in the twenty-first century doesn't make it easy to choose intentional solitude, humans have struggled with this choice for hundreds of years. In the sixth century B.C.E., the Chinese philosopher Lao Tzu wrote,

> There is no need to run outside
> for better seeing,
> nor to peer from a window. Rather abide
> at the center of your being;
> For the more you leave it, the less you learn.
> Search your heart and see
> If he is wise who takes each turn:
> The way to do is to be.[7]

Chapter Five

Make Boundaries

Things which matter most must never be
at the mercy of things which matter least.
—*Attributed to Goethe*

One of the times I have carved out for writing is Thursday mornings, which means I don't schedule clients or other appointments until the afternoon; I let the answering machine field phone calls; I leave breakfast dishes in the sink, and so on. After my time-in, my computer and I have a steady date on Thursdays.

But this morning when I awoke, I looked out to a bright, blue-skied, incredibly inviting spring morning—this after a New England winter that rivaled any in my memory for longest, coldest, and snowiest—and somehow I found myself outside needing to check on some seedlings I had planted. When I came back in, being in a plants-and-flowers frame of mind, I noticed that several of my indoor plants were calling out for water. "Well," I thought, "it'll just take a minute to give them some water, and really, they *need* water. I shouldn't let them get any drier." The phone rang while I was watering; I knew my mother would be calling to make arrangements for dinner, so I decided to get that little piece of business out of the way before getting to the computer. Surprise! It wasn't my mother; it was my freshman-year college roommate whom I hadn't spoken to in thirty years. Needless to say, we had a little catching up to do, so by the time I sat down for my "steady" date with the computer, it was after 11 o'clock.

My experience this morning is an example of a small, relatively benign slice of life without boundaries. Making boundaries has to do with saying "no" to what we *don't* want or *don't* mean to do, in order to say "yes" to what we *do* want or *do* mean to do. Making boundaries is a fundamental Deep River skill. We need boundaries in order to slow down, to take time-in, and to stay centered and on course in daily life. Without them, we're constantly in response mode—as I was earlier today—which is an unsatisfying and ineffective way to live. I responded to the beautiful day by going outside (an alternative would have been to plan a walk for later in the day), then I responded to the dry indoor plants as if they wouldn't survive another minute without water. By then, response mode had fully kicked in, which made it seem natural to pick up the phone, even though I normally don't at that time of day. Responding to the ring of the phone by answering it resulted in a thirty-minute diversion rather than the two-minute call I'd expected. Talking to my old roommate was something I *did* want to do, but it didn't need to happen in the middle of my writing time. By the time I sat down at the computer, not only had I lost a significant chunk of time but I had also lost something less obvious but perhaps more significant: the energy generated when my actions are aligned with my intentions—that is, when I do what I mean to do, and don't do what I don't mean to do.

Let me address a common misconception about making boundaries. The need to say "no" to certain people or things at certain times does not mean that responding or saying "yes" is bad. Our ability to respond to the people in our lives and to events in our world, as well as to the beauty of a spring day, is one of the gifts of being human. In creating boundaries, we are not seeking to negate our ability to react or respond; we are seeking balance. As women, most of us were socialized early in our lives to respond to others' needs on demand, but we had precious little training in how to set boundaries and say "no." Anne Lindbergh warns of the effect of constantly being in response mode. She writes, "Woman today is tending more and more toward the state William James describes so well in the German word 'Zerrissenheit—torn-to-pieces-hood.' She cannot live perpetually in 'Zerrissenheit.' She will be shattered into a thousand pieces. On the contrary, she must consciously encourage those pursuits which oppose the centrifugal forces of today."[1] The ability to make boundaries is a key antidote to the fragmented experience of Zerrissenheit, as Annie's story illustrates.

Annie's Story: Making Boundaries, Finding Joy

When I first met Annie, I would say that "torn-to-pieces-hood" was a good way to describe the state she was in most of the time. She owned a small retail store and ran her interior design business out of it. She worked ten- to twelve-hour days, including weekends, squeezing in her work for clients around store hours. In addition, Annie was available to her clients by cell phone any time, day or night. She was struggling financially, partly because the retail business had suffered as a result of a downturn in the economy. But as Annie and I looked more closely, we saw that she was also struggling because she was not billing for all her hours, in some cases so much so that she was essentially giving her services away. Because she was working such long hours, just about all self-care had gone out the window. She was getting no exercise, too little sleep, and barely taking time to eat. Despite her desperately overpacked work schedule, Annie always managed to respond to requests from friends. When a friend wanted to talk or needed some design advice, pet sitting, or even help moving furniture, Annie was there. Needless to say, the word "no" was not big in her vocabulary.

She says of her life at that time, "I didn't understand boundaries. I was trying to please everyone all the time, and I think I was feeling angry and taken advantage of, although I didn't realize it. I would go into a friend's house, and if it was dirty, I would clean it. If it was somebody's birthday that I didn't know well, I would spend more money than I could afford on a gift. I thought if I went that extra mile for everybody, I would be noticed more, accepted more. In the meantime, I was feeling used, invisible, and just worn down."

Reining in her tendency to give too much and learning how to make boundaries was a gradual process for Annie. Once she saw more clearly what she was doing and understood the need to set limits, she began to practice. "In every interaction with people, I practiced not going overboard, not doing or saying too much, learning to be quiet, asking myself, 'OK, what do *I* want here?'"

After several small victories, she had a big victory in making a boundary at work. She explained, "I had a client who wanted to invite another interior designer to a meeting. I told her I didn't think it was a good idea, that it was like having two creative directors involved with one film, but I agreed to do it. When we met, this other designer wanted all of the information I had researched—and I said 'no, I don't think that's appropriate.' After the meeting ended, I left the room and thought, 'Whew! Who said *that*?!' It was a great feeling. I had protected myself, respected myself. The feeling was, 'I'm a person too. I matter.'"

One of the obstacles Annie had to overcome in making boundaries was her guilt. She says,

> Before, I did everything out of guilt, not wanting to hurt anyone's feelings. I was so used to the guilt that I didn't recognize it. Now, when I notice it, I ask myself, "What am I feeling bad about? Should I be?" (I talk to myself a lot now!) I question the guilt and don't just assume it's warranted. And a lot of the time, it's not! For example, recently a man asked me out, and I found out that he was married. I didn't want to hurt his feelings—even though he was married! It was really hard for me to say "no," but I did. When I say "no" now in situations like that, the guilt stings for a moment, and then I feel great afterward. I feel really happy because I can stand up for myself.

After about a year of practice with making boundaries, Annie decided to close her store and have one instead of two full-time jobs. This choice was another step in including her needs in the picture. A few months after the store closed, she said, "My life is so much easier. It's more sane, more balanced. I'm not trying to please everybody and be perfect all the time. I'm not always asking, 'What can I do for you? Want me to shine your shoes?'"

The Many Benefits of Making Boundaries

Annie's story shows that making boundaries is not a peripheral or insignificant part of the process of slowing down and reclaiming our lives. For Annie, learning to say "no" was a thread woven again and again through the fabric of her new, more balanced and satisfying lifestyle. Each time she set an appropriate boundary, the statement "I'm a person too" was strengthened. And as that feeling got stronger, it became easier to make choices that weren't based solely on making sure she pleased others; she now had the freedom to ask herself, "What do *I* want?" And although she still wrestled with guilt some of the time when she made choices based on her own wants and needs, she also felt and saw the benefits of this new way of being. She was no longer running herself ragged at the beck and call of clients. She brought exercise back into her week and took time to shop for food and cook for herself. And for the first time in years, she took a much-needed and deeply renewing one-week vacation.

Gradually, Annie made a crucial shift in her thinking about setting boundaries: she moved from the belief that saying "no" was selfish to the knowledge that saying "no" was an affirmation of self. For Annie, as for the rest of us, saying "yes" when we want to say "no" drains energy and results in our feeling powerless and resentful. On the other hand, saying "no" when we mean no indicates self-respect and can be empowering. It is a natural expression of the understanding that, as Annie put it, "I'm a person too." That is, I am neither more important nor less important than everyone else.

When Annie first began to ask, "What do I want?" she also did a lot of asking herself, "Am I becoming self-absorbed?" A couple of insights helped her answer this question. One was the realization that a lot of what she had thought of as her compassionate acts were really attempts to get people to appreciate her. Her caring was not entirely selfless, but in fact contained a little disguised self-absorption. The other insight came from her understanding that wanting things for herself didn't negate her true caring for other people. Taking her own needs into account was simply a way to include herself in the picture. As she said, "I deserve certain things, just like everybody else does. For the longest time, I didn't think I deserved anything. I think I'm actually *more* caring now, and that includes caring toward myself. Buying food, for example. I would buy the bare minimum. Now, I not only buy food, I buy flowers for myself. I'm not just surviving; I'm living and taking joy in my life, and I'm grateful for every part of it."

In addition to feeling more gratitude and compassion, Annie experienced another unexpected effect of learning to set boundaries. She noticed that she was more relaxed and open with people, which she didn't understand at first. As we talked, she saw two reasons for her new openness. First, saying "yes" when she meant to say "no" often created resentment or anger within herself, which made her close down. Second, she saw that without the ability to set limits, she had put up a subtle but ever-present emotional wall, protecting her from being swept away by other people's needs and agendas. The more she trusted herself to set limits when she needed to, the less she needed the all-encompassing protection of the wall. Recently, she described an image she has—perfect for an interior designer—of what has replaced the wall now that she can make boundaries:

> I visualize a screen around my body, like a screen porch. It's like one of those very inviting screen porches with natural wood and comfortable wicker chairs with thick green cushions. But the screening is a perfectly round circle all the way around me; I think that's about my being a whole person. The screen isn't a barrier; it's very thin and perforated. And it has a really nice screen door. So when people come to me now, I can allow them in, but I first have to ask myself, "Is this safe for me? Is this what I want?" And if it is, then I open the door. I can allow people in now, but in a safe way.

Saying "No" to Stuff

One of my all-time favorite cartoons, by Robert Mankoff, shows a man at his desk, talking on the phone while checking his datebook.

The caption reads, "No—Thursday's out. How about never—is never good for you?"[2] Women in my groups love this cartoon; it comes right out and says what we would never dare but often wish we could say. For many of us, like Annie, our most difficult challenge is saying "no" to people. Both the "Blocking Beliefs" section and the exercises at the end of this chapter address ways to work with this challenge, perhaps in a slightly less blunt way than the cartoon suggests! But in addition, in our consumer-driven, achievement-oriented culture of speed, interruption, and distraction, we need boundaries in such arenas as time, space, work, noise, technology, events, stuff. There are so many opportunities to learn how to say "no"!

Have you ever noticed that the things on your to-do list can exert a palpable force on your attention? One very ordinary day when my children were younger, I had a small epiphany about making boundaries. I was tired after a busy day and the kids were both at friends' houses, so I decided to sit in the living room for a few quiet moments before making dinner. There was a basket of unfolded laundry sitting on the living room floor. As I sat, I noticed a very strange thing—the laundry was pulling me to fold it. Or so it seemed. It was as if there was an invisible thread from me to the laundry basket, and even though I had chosen to relax and sit quietly, part of me was already in motion toward folding laundry. I found myself saying "no"—out loud!— to the unfolded clothes, and consciously pulling my attention away from the basket and back to myself.

In the living room that day, I became more conscious of the need to set clear boundaries not just with people in my life but with the many other chores and responsibilities that call out to me. That awareness has helped me to notice when I am being pulled by things I don't mean to attend to immediately. Again, a clear "no" makes for a more wholehearted "yes." By saying "no" to the laundry, I was able to fully enter into a few moments of quiet, which actually did provide some renewal before I began making dinner.

So what kinds of things might we say "no" to? Once we start looking, we may see a great many possibilities. Like Annie, another client named Barbara was working on setting better boundaries at home and at work. One of Barbara's "laundry baskets" was the flood of catalogues that arrived in her mailbox—some requested, many unbidden—every day. When she began looking at what she wanted to say "no" to in order to make more time for herself, she realized that there were only a very few catalogues that she actually ordered from. The rest she found herself looking through simply because they had arrived in her home. Not only did they create substantial clutter, but the catalogues also wasted Barbara's precious time; she didn't really mean to spend it looking at pages of things she didn't need. Barbara said "no" with a catalogue-reduction campaign. For the next month, instead of looking through the catalogues she didn't want, she called the customer service number as soon as they arrived and asked to be taken off the company's mailing list. The call took less time than leafing through the pages and resulted in less clutter and more free time.

Mary, a musician who practiced at home, put a chair blocking the kitchen door so she wouldn't be tempted to start cleaning instead of playing her instrument. Ingrid, who lived in a first-floor apartment, bought a pair of soundproofing headphones to block out distracting street noise on the days she worked at home. Celia wanted to put a boundary around what she called her "addiction" to checking the latest news on the Internet several times a day. She decided to set up two designated news check-ins, once in the morning and once in the afternoon, leaving her more time to do what she intended to do at the computer during the rest of the day.

We all get drawn into unplanned activities, some of which, in hindsight, we can see were not worth our time and energy. Choice is the key. Are you *choosing* to watch television when you do, listen to the radio, answer the phone, surf the Internet, check your e-mail, stay up later at night, stay at work later in the day, take on more volunteer "opportunities," buy more clothes (or jewelry, furniture, toys, books, beauty products)? The goal is not to become rigid and over-plan our lives. But if we are in the habit of responding to whatever calls out for our attention in any moment, we are likely to be fragmented in our daily lives and distracted from what really matters to us. Boundaries help us to do more of what we mean to do, more of the time. They help us resist the tendency to scatter our energy too far and wide, or as Anne Lindbergh describes it, to take our pitchers and attempt to water a field, not a garden.[3]

Saying "No" to Too Many Good Things

We can easily recognize the need to say "no" to things that waste our time. It's harder to accept the idea of too many good things. We get overscheduled and torn-to-pieces not just by the things we *have* to do but by the things we *want* to do. I have a friend who used to describe herself as a "meaning junkie." She said "yes" to any opportunity for deep, meaningful, growthful experiences. This included workshops, trips, courses, and talks by spiritual teachers, as well as purchases of books, tapes, and other paraphernalia that she associated with enhancing meaning in her life. Each of these things had value, but choosing *all* of them, she came to realize, was straining her time, energy, and pocketbook. She likened her overindulgence in these experiences to eating a meal with too much rich food: it no longer nourishes; rather, it makes us feel sick. After actually getting sick with a stress-related digestive condition that laid her low for a few weeks, my friend began to say "no" to some of these tempting opportunities for growth, leaving herself more time to digest the meaningful experiences she did choose.

Making Boundaries to Take Time-In

Time management expert Stephen Covey has a helpful way of reminding us to "put first things first" (one of his seven habits of highly effective people). His time management matrix has four quadrants that represent four categories of activity.[4] The time evaluation matrix included here is adapted from Covey's diagram.

Quadrant I includes activities that are both urgent and important—that is, pressing, immediate problems or crises such as a hurt child needing medical attention or a major work deadline. I'll discuss Quadrant II shortly.

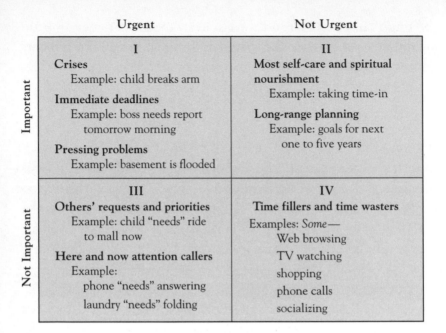

	Urgent	Not Urgent

Important	**I**
	Crises
	    Example: child breaks arm
	Immediate deadlines
	    Example: boss needs report
	       tomorrow morning
	Pressing problems
	    Example: basement is flooded
		II
		Most self-care and spiritual
		nourishment
		    Example: taking time-in
		Long-range planning
		    Example: goals for next
		       one to five years

Not Important	**III**
	Others' requests and priorities
	    Example: child "needs" ride
	       to mall now
	Here and now attention callers
	    Example:
	       phone "needs" answering
	       laundry "needs" folding
		IV
		Time fillers and time wasters
		Examples: *Some*—
		    Web browsing
		    TV watching
		    shopping
		    phone calls
		    socializing

Time Evaluation Matrix

Source: Adapted from Stephen R. Covey, *The 7 Habits of Highly Effective People* (New York: Simon & Schuster, 1989), p. 151.

Quadrant III represents activities that are urgent but not truly important. For example, a ringing phone or a child asking for a ride to a friend's house are urgent in the sense that they are demanding immediate attention, but they are not necessarily important. Many phone calls, though perhaps they are important to the person who is calling, are not so important that you need to respond at that moment. Likewise with the request for a ride: something that is important to someone else is not necessarily important to you at that moment. Covey says that people who spend a lot of time in Quadrant III, dealing with what's urgent but not important, *think* they're reacting to things that are both urgent and important. But in fact, both the sense of urgency and the importance of these matters are often based on others' priorities or expectations and not necessarily on their own.

Quadrant IV includes activities that are neither important nor urgent. Barbara's catalogue reading would fit here. The activities that we ourselves label as "wasting time" fit here. Busywork fits here. It's a very rare television program indeed that doesn't belong in this quadrant.

Quadrant II: What Falls Off the List

I saved Quadrant II for last, because the activities that belong in this quadrant are the ones that most often fall off the to-do list. They are the important but not urgent activities. They take some intention to make happen, and therefore they *don't* happen when we're in response mode—that is, when we are responding to the urgent matters of the moment. They include activities of self-care, long-range planning and prioritizing, and spiritual nourishment. They are the activities that we know would be beneficial but that many of us never or rarely get around to.

Time-in, one of the fundamental Deep River practices, is a Quadrant II activity. It is the kind of time we need in order to get our priorities straight, to remember what it is we truly want to say "yes" to in our lives. It is important but not urgent, and therefore, if we don't make boundaries to protect it, time-in can very easily get crowded out of the daily schedule. To invite meaning, depth, and balance into our lives through taking time-in, we may need to say no to both people and things.

Scheduling Time-In

My time-in is in the morning. To say "yes" to time-in, I learned to say "no" to scheduling clients early in the morning, to reading the paper, washing breakfast dishes, and answering phone calls. All of these things can happen at other times of the day, but in order to put them off, I needed to recognize the importance of my Deep River time and to protect it by saying "no" to other, often urgent (that is, right in front of me—like the dirty dishes) but not important activities. The boundaryless experience described at the beginning of this chapter shows that I sometimes fail at *maintaining* the boundaries I have set for myself. But *making* a boundary for any Quadrant II activity makes it much more likely to happen and also easier to come back to when I get sidetracked.

If you have difficulty taking time-in regularly, it might be helpful to give some thought to what you need to say "no" to in order to say a more wholehearted "yes" to this renewing time for yourself. Making boundaries around time-in is a good way to build your "no muscle." (We will work on this in the exercise called "Finding Your Inner Boundary Maker," which appears later in this chapter.)

Laurel, a financial adviser, found that her "no muscle" had developed considerably when she came back to work after a long series of treatments for breast cancer. She told her boss that three times a week from noon to one, she would be taking a yoga class across the street. This was her time for renewal; she was very clear that she needed it, both for her well-being and for her ability to perform well at her job. Laurel was able to communicate the value of taking this break in a way that resulted in her time-in being supported. Coming back from an illness can give us a perspective on what really matters, which in turn makes it easier to protect time for important but not urgent activities such as, in Laurel's case, her yoga class. Our goal, though, is to learn how to claim time for renewal and self-care before we are faced with a life-or-death situation.

I have seen women find creative ways to say "no" to children, spouses, friends, relatives, bosses, coworkers, pets, e-mail, telephones, work demands, housecleaning, bed making, cooking, puttering, carpooling, bill paying, you name it, in order to be able to take some quiet time for themselves. Again, this doesn't mean not responding to people we care about or shirking responsibilities; it means not being driven unceasingly by our responsibilities to other people and things to the detriment of our own sanity.

Many women have found, to their surprise, that they can explain time-in to their children and, depending on the age and temperament of the child, get cooperation and sometimes interest in their taking time for reflection. One mother explained a little about meditation to her four- and six-year-old kids and then had them make a sign for her bedroom door that said, "Mummy is meditating." She explains, "They wanted to try meditating, which lasted all of about forty-five seconds! But they knew that for the fifteen minutes that the sign was on the door, they wouldn't disturb me unless there was an emergency." Another mom explained to her four year-old, who understood that a store is either open or closed for business, that for ten minutes at her chosen time, "Mommy's closed."

So there are many ways to create time for time-in. Generally speaking, no one is going to hand it to you; you have to set boundaries and claim it. In *Women Who Run with the Wolves*, Clarissa Estés says of time spent "going home" (her name for time-in), "Regardless of your home time, an hour or days, remember, other people can pet your cats even though your cats say only you can do it right. . . . The grass will get a little brown but it will revive. You and your child will miss each other, but be glad when you return. Your mate may grump. They'll get over it. Your boss may threaten. She or he will get over it too. Staying overlong is madness. Going home is sanity."[5]

Blocking Belief: "If I say 'no,' people won't love me."

We tend to think of ourselves as one undivided, whole person. While in one way this is true, at the same time, we all have multiple aspects or parts of our personalities. The belief "If I say 'no,' people won't love me," like most other blocking beliefs, usually arises from a *part* of us. We might notice these parts, or subpersonalities, most easily when they are in conflict.[6] For example, the social part of me might think, "I'd really like to go out tonight," while the shy part might be thinking, "No way. I'd like to stay home with a good book." We might notice subpersonalities in other people when they shift from one part to another—for example, when we observe someone who is reserved with coworkers become warm and effusive with a pet.

Each of our inner parts has its own particular behaviors, beliefs, gifts, skills, and needs. For example, in telling Annie's story, I focused on what she called her "pleaser" part, who is generous to a fault and has difficulty setting boundaries. I didn't mention that Annie also is a risk taker in her creative life, has a strong sense of adventure that has led her to travel widely, and is an accomplished pianist. These are skills and attitudes that belong to parts of her other than the pleaser.

When Annie and I began to examine what made her pleaser part tick, she saw that the belief "If I say 'no,' people won't love me" clearly belonged to this part. Identifying the subpersonality that holds a particular blocking belief is helpful because once we see that a *part* within us holds that belief, we can call on other parts that have the capacity to see things differently. For example, Annie's pleaser part began when she was a six-year-old girl who did everything she could think of to please her parents and pull some attention away from her newborn sister. Once she identified the subpersonality that needed to constantly do for others, she was able to step back, away from this part and into a more adult self. She discovered that her adult self had a quiet confidence that surprised her. Annie was delighted to find that this adult self, unlike the six-year-old pleaser subpersonality, could say "no" effortlessly and, in fact, found saying "no" when she meant no to be much simpler than the complicated dance of trying to please.

❧ Exercise: Finding Your Inner Boundary Maker

Working with subpersonalities is a valuable tool for promoting self-understanding and reducing inner conflict. This exercise is a brief introduction to one of the many ways that subpersonality work can benefit our relationship to ourselves and others. (For a more in-depth exploration of subpersonality work, see the references on psychosynthesis in the Selected Reading.) If you fear that people will go away or you will lose love if you say "no," I invite you to read through and then try the brief visualization that follows. By visualizing what our subpersonalities look like—getting an image of them in our mind's eye—we create a means to understand them better, observe and dialogue with them imaginally, and improve our relationship with them. Annie, for example, visualized the pleaser as a self-effacing young girl. Once she could see this part in her imagination, she realized that it was young and insecure, and she was able to reassure the pleaser when the adult part of her needed to say "no."

1. Close your eyes, take a couple of deep breaths, and allow your attention to move inward. Now ask yourself, *"Who inside me believes I won't be loved if I say 'no'?"* Let an image come to mind that represents this part. Try not to censor the image; just allow whatever comes. It might be an image of yourself at a different age or of a person—male or female—that isn't you. It might be a metaphorical image—an animal, a natural or man-made object, or even a cartoon character. Take your time to see what image comes to you. Notice what this part looks like, where it is, what it is doing. Observe your image, and see what it has to show you. (Pause and take your time.) Can you ask it what it needs? See if you can hear or sense what it needs. (Again, pause and take your time.) Is there something you could say or do to give this part what it needs?

   Take all the time you need. If you want to, you can write down or draw what you have seen in your mind's eye before going on to the next step.

2. Close your eyes, and again allow your attention to move inward. Now ask yourself, *"Who inside me has the ability to set appropriate boundaries?"* In your mind's eye, see a part of you that can make appropriate boundaries with people. If you don't think you have such a part, assume for now that this part exists in you, even if you've never been aware of it. Let an image arise in your imagination that represents this part. Take your time. Try not to censor the image; just allow whatever comes. It could be a person, an animal, an object or something else. If no image comes to mind, think of a person, real or fictional, whom you admire for being able to set good boundaries. You can use the image of this person as your inner boundary maker.

   When you have an image of the part of you that can make boundaries, notice what it looks like and what quality or qualities it possesses. Take your time. Observe your image, and see what it has to show you. What does this part believe, understand, or demonstrate to you about setting boundaries and saying "no"? (Pause and take your time.) Is there anything it might do or say to help the part that is afraid that saying "no" means losing love?

Take all the time you need. If you want to, you can write down or draw what you have seen in your mind's eye.

Once you have identified the part that fears saying "no" and the part that knows how to say "no," you have inner tools to challenge the belief that making a boundary means losing love. When you notice the fearful part, you can visualize it, turn toward it, and reassure it. You can give it a safe place to be in your imagination while you call forth the part that is able to say "no." If the fear is especially strong and doesn't respond at all to reassurance, you may be dealing with more than you can work with on your own. If so, consider seeking professional help; sometimes a small amount of help from a skilled therapist can go a long way.

Making boundaries with ease takes practice, but the first step— identifying your subpersonalities—can be helpful in itself. The next steps are these: practice, practice, and more practice!

⚜ Exercise: Practicing "No"

Making boundaries gets easier with practice. Strengthening the "no muscle" is like training any muscle: it works best to start with low resistance—that is, setting a boundary that is relatively easy—and work your way gradually to weightier challenges. This exercise may make some space in your calendar and bring more balance into your day, but its primary purpose is to help you *practice* saying "no" and experience the empowerment of choosing to make a boundary.

Once saying "no" comes more easily, the results in the flow of your daily life and in your ability to receive nourishment from the Deep River will follow.

1. Use your journal or a sheet of paper to make a list of things to which you currently say "yes" when you would like to say "no." Don't censor this list; that is, don't worry about

   - Whether you are *able* to say "no" at this time
   - Whether you *should* say "no"
   - Whether you would feel guilty saying "no"
   - Whether it is morally correct to say "no"
   - Whether your neighbor, friend, or anyone else says "no"

   Just include on your list anything that is in the category of "currently saying yes, but want to say no"—for example,

   - Receiving phone calls at dinnertime
   - Volunteering to help with alumna activities
   - Working through lunch break
   - Watching TV right before bed
   - Having lunch with Jane, who is all talk and no listen

2. Once you have a list of at least ten things, look for the *easiest* thing to say "no" to. Write that one thing at the top of a page, and then think of a small, doable step for making a boundary. It doesn't need to be all or nothing. If you want to say "no" to working through lunch break, you can start by choosing one or two days when you will take a half-hour lunch. If you want to say "no" to certain volunteer requests, you can start by giving yourself time to consider requests ("Let me get back to you about that") rather than saying "yes" or "no" right away.

3. Write your next step in the present tense, as if you have already incorporated it into your life, and be as specific as you can. Examples:

   - On Tuesdays and Thursdays, I take a half-hour lunch break from 1 to 1:30 P.M.

- When people ask me to do something, I never say "yes" immediately. I tell them I'll get back to them, so I have time to decide whether to say "yes" or "no."

4. Discuss or, if you are alone, write in your journal about what obstacles, if any, might get in the way of your next step, and what you can do about them. Examples:

   Obstacle: Sometimes meetings at work go into my planned lunchtime.

   Possible solution: Put the half-hour lunches in my calendar for at least a month in advance as if they are meetings, so I can't schedule other meetings then. When meetings are absolutely unavoidable, schedule in a half-hour break at a different time of that day.

   Obstacle: I get caught up in what I'm doing, lose track of time, and realize later in the day that I haven't stopped or eaten.

   Possible solution: Put lunch breaks in my calendar, remind myself of my intention on the way to work, and set my watch alarm to go off at 12:50 p.m. so that I'll have ten minutes to wrap things up before taking the break.

5. If you can, tell a friend or your Deep River buddy or group what your next step is, what obstacles you foresee, and what you might do about them. It helps to say your plan out loud and get support.

6. Try it out! Record your victories. When you're ready, you can expand this step or choose another item from your list.

———————

Some people by nature are better than others at making boundaries. If this practice is a tough one for you, I encourage you to get support and to think in small steps or, like Talia—a woman in one of my groups—to "think in fairy steps." Talia had a painfully difficult time saying "no." The week before we worked in the group with setting boundaries, her children had created a tiny "fairy village" in the woods near their home, with miniature houses built from sticks and other natural objects. With the image of the fairy village in her mind, when every small step she thought of seemed too big, Talia said, "Maybe if I 'think in fairy steps,' I can do this."

If you need to take fairy steps to practice making boundaries, then know that you are not alone, and count each fairy step as a victory!

Chapter Six

Befriend Feelings

> What would happen if we stopped calling
> painful emotions "negative" and had faith that
> the heart—even in the throes of intense pain—
> can be trusted? . . . The heart heals itself when we
> know how to listen to it. Befriending and mind-
> fully surrendering to our most dreaded emotions,
> we discover the heart's native intelligence.
> —*Miriam Greenspan*,
> Healing Through the Dark Emotions

When I first began offering Deep River groups, I met an acquaintance at the grocery store while I was putting up flyers. I handed her one of the flyers in case she or anyone she knew might be interested. She glanced very briefly at the flyer, saw the word *deep* in the title, and without realizing what she was saying, blurted out, "You wouldn't want to go too deep; you might find out there's nothing there."

That sentiment is just one of many fears about slowing down and looking inward. People keep themselves busy and on the surface of life to avoid all kinds of uncomfortable emotions. "What if I look inside, and I just see emptiness?" "How is my marriage going, really?" "What is this anger (fear, restlessness, grief) about, and will it overwhelm me if I let myself really feel it?" Without slowing down and stepping back, we may not realize how our hectic schedules help us keep our distance from unwanted thoughts and feelings. Busyness is a wonderful defense, and in our culture, we are rewarded for it. The problem is that keeping busy as a way of avoiding or denying uncomfortable feelings eventually reaches a point of diminishing returns. The more we push them down, the more the effort exhausts us and the more those neglected parts of ourselves start turning up the volume in order to be heard. However, if we can *listen to* and *befriend* these disowned feelings rather than push them away, they can become allies rather than enemies. Contrary to what we might fear, these feelings can become part of the rich soil that gives rise to more wholeness in ourselves and more fullness in our lives. Learning to befriend uncomfortable feelings is part of the journey of contacting the Deep River within.

Making Friends with Feelings

In our culture, we are conditioned to distract ourselves or get busy when something disturbs us. Having a job to do, a family to take care of, or some other responsibility that keeps us occupied can certainly be a helpful respite from difficult feelings. So can diversions like watching a movie, turning up the music, going out dancing, or pursuing any enjoyable activity. At times, a healthy distraction is just what we need. However, as a therapist, again and again, I see people come into my office at the point when this approach has stopped working. For them, as for anyone at this point, the next step is usually to *go toward* feelings that they have spent considerable time and effort trying to get away from.

Sometimes the process of turning toward difficult feelings is relatively simple and straightforward. Alice, a client who is a therapist herself, came in one day, furious at her brother. She had learned that he was having an affair and was on the verge of leaving his wife. In Alice's view, he was unnecessarily and foolishly jeopardizing both a good marriage to a good woman and the stability of his children's lives. Alice and her siblings were supposed to take him out that night for his birthday. Although she was close to her brother and wanted to support him, Alice felt so angry at him that she was afraid it would ruin the evening. She was looking for a way to somehow pack the anger away, at least temporarily, so that she could celebrate his birthday.

I suggested that rather than try to distance herself from the anger, even temporarily, she turn toward it. As a therapist, this is just what Alice would have said to one of her own clients, but in wanting to be a good sister and not spoil the party, it hadn't occurred to her to do this herself. To help Alice turn toward her anger, we imagined her brother in a chair across from her, and she expressed her feelings to him, uncensored. This gave her a safe way to allow the angry feelings to surface without doing any harm. As soon as she let herself fully feel the anger, Alice immediately felt sad for her brother and his family but also for herself as a child of divorce. This was not the first time she had touched this sadness, but in staying with it, she considered what it might have been like for her if her parents hadn't gotten a divorce. And for the first time, she saw that there was a silver lining: her parents' divorce, as painful as it was, had loosened up the closed circle of her family and had in fact created more room for her to grow. Alice explained,

> There was a lot of intellectual snobbism in my family. There were a few people accepted into the inner circle, but the vast majority were kept out. Even when we were quite young, when my brother and I had certain friends over, my father and mother would try to convince us that these children were not worthy of us. Once my parents separated, I was able to stop being concerned about who might not be accepted into this family circle, because the family circle didn't exist anymore. This gave me much more freedom to learn how to accept and be comfortable with all different kinds of people.

Toward the end of the session, I asked Alice if what she had just seen and experienced might help her with the anger while at the birthday party that night. Her answer was immediate: "The anger is gone. It was sitting on top of the sadness. . . . As soon as I touched that sadness, the anger completely dissipated." Alice knew she would communicate her view about his choices to her brother at some point, but now she felt that she would be able to do it without fury and that she wouldn't be compelled, out of anger, to do it that night.

Although she needed reminding in that moment, Alice already had considerable experience in allowing and turning toward uncomfortable feelings. For Jenna, another client, this kind of acceptance was entirely new territory. Her story is an example of starting from scratch in learning to go toward and befriend some very uncomfortable feelings. Although the details of her story are particular to Jenna, I tell it here because it illustrates one pathway to becoming more comfortable with difficult emotions. When we find our own unique version of this path, not only does it open up more access to the Deep River realm, but it also helps us begin to befriend and accept all parts of ourselves—the good, the bad, and the ugly. Such acceptance sends broad ripples through our lives, both inner and outer, as we will see in the chapters ahead. But let's begin with Jenna.

Jenna's Story: Making Friends with Fear

Jenna started therapy reluctantly. She had been trying by herself to change a very entrenched pattern of angry, silent withdrawal from her husband, especially in times of stress. "I know at those times that it would help me—and him—if I could reach out, talk to him, and ask for help, but I just can't get myself to do it." She was stuck, and her withdrawal from her husband was taking its toll on her and on the marriage.

At the beginning of our work together, we looked back at Jenna's emotional environment as a child. She had grown up in a family in which it was not OK to express certain feelings. "I learned that I was supposed to suppress the emotions I would label as 'not pretty': sadness, jealousy, fear, for example. I was never comforted or nurtured through those feelings, and I certainly wasn't encouraged to share them. My tendency would be to go in my room and be alone and cry when I was feeling sad, then come out when I felt better." It was helpful for Jenna to understand that she had taken on her parents' negative attitude toward certain feelings. She could also see clearly where her tendency to isolate herself came from, but these insights by themselves didn't help her to change the pattern.

As Jenna became more comfortable in the therapy process and more trusting of me as her guide, we talked about moving beyond mental insight *about* her feelings to actually *feeling* them. At that point, the fear underlying her reluctance to come to therapy surfaced. She later described it this way: "I was so afraid of what I would find. I had this inherent assumption that there was something really bad inside, some big black hole, and that if I started the journey to explore it, I would be overwhelmed. I would put a toe in and get sucked down into a whirlpool and not be able to get out. I thought if I started to feel the feelings I'd been avoiding for so long even just a little bit, that was *all* I was going to be able to feel. I was afraid I'd be completely consumed by them."

Not long after Jenna named this fear, the opportunity to feel the most uncomfortable of her feelings presented itself in an unexpected way. Jenna came in one week and shared a stressful incident with one of her children. After she talked for a while, something in her body language led me to ask her, "How are you feeling right now?" There was an unusually long silence. As we learned through the rest of our time that day and over the next several sessions, this silence was not simply a pause to find the right words to name her feelings. My question had acted as a sort of trigger that sent her into a frozen state in which she lost touch with herself and with me and felt unable to speak.[1] This frozen state was familiar to Jenna; she had experienced it as a child and as a young adult, and it was a terrifying feeling that she wanted to avoid at all costs. She described it, once she could speak again, this way: "When you ask how I'm feeling, a wall goes up right away, and it's like I'm trapped by myself behind the wall. I feel very small, and my breathing is tight; everything is tight. I feel like I'm sinking and I can't ask for help."

With a great deal of emphasis from me on safety and on going at her own pace and in small steps, Jenna began to turn toward this feeling that she had tried to keep at a distance for so long. It was difficult to avoid in therapy because just asking her how she was feeling usually triggered it, but that also gave us the opportunity to explore it. When it came up, we tried various ways of easing the fear. I stayed in contact with her, talked her through it, had her open her eyes and ground herself in the physical reality of the room where we were sitting. I reassured her that though this feeling was old and powerful, we were in an entirely different and safe environment. After one session in which she experienced this frozen state, Jenna recalled an experience from childhood that she hadn't remembered for a long time but that she realized was linked to the fear and her reaction. When she was about nine, she had been the object of a thirteen-year-old neighborhood boy's sexual experimentation. "He tried things on me, and then he'd ask me how it felt." Jenna had been scared and confused by the incident but hadn't felt safe enough in her family to share this "not pretty" experience and so had simply kept silent. Her reaction to the experience at the time—being paralyzed, feeling vulnerable, and having no voice—was the same set of feelings she was having in my office.

Jenna's early experience was echoed many times in her sexual encounters as a teenager and a young adult. "If I was in a situation where I wasn't comfortable with what was going on, I couldn't speak up for myself. Instead, I'd feel really awkward and uncomfortable. All my attention would go toward the panic associated with these feelings, and the way it froze my ability to speak. I couldn't say, 'I don't want to do this right now,' so I would say nothing, and it would happen, and I'd feel victimized. Then afterward, I'd feel really bad about myself because I kept putting myself in this kind of situation. I didn't have the tools to get out of the freeze zone."

Eventually, Jenna did develop the tools she needed to get out of the freeze zone. Paradoxically, as she understands it now, the key to getting out of it was the ability to allow it. "After the fear and paralysis happened a number of times in your office, and it felt bad but it *did* end, I started to have just a little bit of space around it so that I could actually begin to talk to you while I was in it, and I also could say to myself and believe, 'I'll come out of this.' Then I began to be able to guide myself to *stay* there, and reassure myself, give myself a sense of safety. The freezing up still happens to me sometimes, but it's so different, because when I feel the beginning of it—just a little discomfort—I don't panic. The fear of what I might feel next used to throw me further into it. Now I notice the discomfort and the edge of fear, but I'm not trying to push it the hell away as fast as I can. And that makes more space, and it's OK." She sums up her new understanding this way: "It's so non-intuitive. You assume that if you push the fear away, it'll get smaller, not bigger. But actually if you push it away, it gets bigger, and if you let it stay, it remains small."

Jenna's newfound ability to befriend this difficult feeling gave her more trust in herself. She now knew how to experience internal discomfort and not react with the panicked feeling of "I can't handle this." Going *toward* the feeling and exploring it rather than pushing it away also resulted in new compassion for herself. "I used to be so angry at myself for making the same mistake over and over again. Now I really know that I couldn't just choose for that paralysis not to happen. And I have a sense of compassion and forgiveness for myself."

With more compassion toward herself, the vague sense that "there's something really bad inside" began to dissolve, and this in turn made it much easier to reach out to her husband when she was feeling stressed and "not pretty." "Now I don't just get angry and withdraw. I can say what's going on with me and ask him for help."

In addition to this needed shift in her relationship with her husband, there was another benefit of Jenna's inner work that she hadn't expected: it opened the door to taking time-in. Jenna had learned to meditate as a college student but had never been able to sustain the practice. Now she understood why meditation, which involved sitting still, being with herself, and allowing whatever feelings and sensations arose, had been so hard for her. For the first time, she felt safe enough to attend a weekend meditation retreat and take up a consistent meditation practice.

What Does It Mean to Befriend Difficult Feelings?

American Buddhist nun Pema Chödrön notes, "As a species, we should never underestimate our low tolerance for discomfort."[2] Nonetheless, as Jenna's story illustrates, it truly is possible to learn to move toward uncomfortable feelings, and we benefit, sometimes in unexpected ways, by doing so. In some cases, just becoming aware of a tendency to move away from feelings and understanding why befriending them is valuable are enough to prompt you to begin trying something different. Depending on what your history is, what your current life is like, and what issues you are facing, you may be able to do this process on your own or, like Jenna, you may need help. The exercise at the end of this chapter will guide you in this process of befriending your emotions. If you read it over and it seems doable rather than daunting, then give it a try on your own. If, as you read it, you sense some part or parts of you putting on the brakes, throwing up red flags, or otherwise resisting the idea vigorously, listen to yourself. Trust your instincts and your own sense of timing. Consider getting some help; sometimes the help of a friend is enough, while in other cases, professional help is called for. If you have a history of trauma or depression or if you are concerned about any other mental health issue, it would be wise to seek professional help, especially if the practice of going toward feelings is new to you.[3]

The key to befriending feelings is an attitude of acceptance that is, for most of us, an unfamiliar way of relating to discomfort of any kind. But it is possible to cultivate this kind of acceptance, as a member of one of my Deep River groups taught us. When Lynn came to the group, she had already been meditating for many years. She provided a model for other group members who were struggling with how to manage difficult emotions as they practiced taking time-in. Lynn said, "Every time I sit down to meditate—*every single time*—I hit a layer of sadness. I'm used to it now; I know it will be there, I feel it as I begin to get quiet, and eventually I move down through it. I know now that it's just a layer of feeling and I don't have to be afraid of it. I can allow it, and that lets me allow other feelings, including a sense of peace that's often somehow underneath the sadness."

With the help of her meditation practice, Lynn had come to accept this sadness, neither making it bigger than it was nor trying to avoid it or make it go away. In my experience, this befriending, or "unconditional friendliness," as it's called in Buddhism, is the most helpful attitude we can cultivate toward difficult feelings. Befriending does not necessarily mean enjoying or loving or even liking a particular emotional state. It means allowing that emotion to be as it is, not judging it, not analyzing it, not trying to change, control, resist, or deny it, minimize it, repress it, indulge it, or act it out. Of course, true acceptance, allowing things to be as they are, is easier said than done. When a wave of intense grief or sometimes even just the slightest hint of the restlessness associated with fear passes through us, most of us are so quick to look for a fix that we don't even realize what we're doing. We get busy, have a drink, call a friend, eat a cookie—whatever it takes to get that feeling to subside, to numb it, get some distance from it. Over time, we develop a habit of going away from uncomfortable feelings. As when breaking any habit, effort and practice are needed to unlearn this method of coping.

Miriam Greenspan, in her wise book *Healing Through the Dark Emotions*, says, "Our emotional illiteracy has less to do with our inability to subdue negative emotions than it does with our inability to authentically and mindfully *feel* them."[4] This is an important point. It's obvious that when we suppress, repress, or otherwise distance ourselves from a feeling, we are not befriending it. But befriending *also* does not mean indulging our feelings. To authentically and mindfully feel an emotion is not the same as acting it out. Pema Chödrön gives an amusing description of what happens when we indulge feelings:

> A simple feeling will arise, and instead of simply letting it be there, we panic. . . . Instead of just sitting in some kind of openness with our uncomfortable feeling, we bring out the bellows and fan away at it. With our thoughts and emotions, we keep it inflamed, hot; we won't let it go. . . . We enlarge the feeling and march it down the street with banners that proclaim how bad everything is. We knock on every door asking people to sign petitions until there is a whole army of people who agree with us that everything is wrong.[5]

If Alice, who was angry at her brother's infidelity, had simply acted out her anger rather than stopping to turn toward it and listen to it, her brother's birthday might have been memorable, but not in a good way. Not acting out the anger didn't mean not expressing her opinions when the time was right; Alice was confident that her brother would be much more receptive to her view of his situation once she could communicate with concern rather than anger. If she had simply indulged her anger, she also would not have been able to hear and receive the underlying message of sadness, which gave her a new and healing perspective on her past.

So befriending a feeling means neither indulging nor repressing a feeling, nor trying to manipulate it in any way. Rather, it means pausing when we notice an emotion, and letting it be; we breathe with it, give it some space in our awareness, and actually *feel* it. We notice the body sensations that naturally accompany feelings. (When we are trying to manage or manipulate our emotions, we can lose sight of the fact that they are, first and foremost, energies that live in the body.) And in this process of allowing and attending to feelings without judgment or manipulation, we can actually receive the information and energy that our emotions have to offer us. Greenspan explains the purpose of the dark emotions of grief, fear, and despair: "Their purpose is not to make us miserable, drive us crazy, or shame, weaken, or defeat us, but to teach us about ourselves, others, and the world, to open our hearts to compassion, to help us heal and change our lives. They bring us information and supply us with energy—the raw material of spiritual empowerment and transformation."[6] For emotions to be this kind of fuel, we need to have the capacity to go toward them and, as Jenna learned, to allow them space in our awareness and in our bodies.

Uncomfortable "Positive" Feelings

It's commonly assumed that the difficult feelings are the "negative" ones, but many people find "positive" feelings uncomfortable, too. For Kristen, who had a lifelong pattern of attending to others' needs and neglecting her own, one of the biggest challenges has been learning to tolerate praise, appreciation, or just about any kind of positive attention. She even described receiving birthday presents as "painful" and, at times, "excruciating." As she began to feel better about herself, she was better able to receive positive attention from others and not immediately extinguish positive feelings that arose from that attention or from other events and experiences. Kristen's discomfort with "good" feelings was unusually strong, but for many of us, positive feelings may touch a place of unworthiness inside or call attention to a painful baseline lack of love or happiness that we don't want to be reminded of. For these and other reasons, we may deflect, minimize, or push away the very feelings that can nourish those hungry places. If this is so for you, learning to befriend love, joy, and gratitude are as much a part of the journey of touching the Deep River as befriending grief, fear, and despair.

Beliefs That Block Us from Befriending Feelings

"We weren't born with our bias against the dark emotions," says Miriam Greenspan. "We can change what we believe and how we react to grief, fear, and despair . . . and begin to taste the freedom and power of letting our emotions be."[7]

Several common beliefs in what Greenspan calls our "emotion-phobic" culture fuel the habit of trying to *not feel* certain feelings. As you read the beliefs that follow, see if one or more of them describes a mental obstacle that you have been holding, perhaps unconsciously, about your own feelings. If none of these applies to you, perhaps reading them will help you think about and clarify what beliefs about feelings you might be holding, if any, that are obstacles to befriending your emotions.

Blocking Belief: "If I open the door to the feelings I've been avoiding, I'll be overwhelmed and consumed by them."

When we hold this very common belief, we fear that if we allow ourselves to feel our dark emotions, they will be as large and destructive as a tidal wave. In fact, the fear that certain feelings will be overwhelming is often strengthened by our efforts to ignore those difficult feelings or push them away. This dynamic is similar to that of a parent dealing with a child who gets louder and more out of control the more she is told to wait, wait, wait: the louder the child gets, the more the parent assumes that the child's needs will take too much time and energy. In fact, when the parent turns attention *toward* the child, she calms down and her demands become manageable. Likewise, when we turn our attention toward a feeling that we've been ignoring, it becomes *more* manageable, not less.

Blocking Belief: "If I let myself feel the feelings I've been avoiding, that's all I'll be able to feel; they'll take over and I'll lose control of my life."

This is the all-or-nothing belief about emotions. Either I lock them away, or they will take over my life. Either I rule them, or they will rule me. The antidote here is the principle of small steps discussed in Chapter Three. We can practice allowing an uncomfortable feeling in small doses, going toward it, and then choosing to move away from it. As Jenna learned, her psyche was already very skilled at distancing her from the paralyzed feeling, and she didn't have to give that skill up as she practiced going toward the discomfort: "It took me quite a few visits to trust that I could go inside, feel those feelings, and then walk out and have the rest of my day and not be completely overwhelmed."

Blocking Belief: "If I let myself feel the feelings I've avoided, I'll have to change my life—now!"

An example of this belief in operation might sound like this: "If I let myself feel how unhappy I am in my marriage, I'll have to leave." The underlying assumption is that our feelings, if we allow them, will take over completely and will fully and immediately determine our actions. In fact, we still have our mind and our ability to make informed choices and measured changes. Our feelings give us more information—often, very valuable information—to help shape those choices, but they don't necessarily enforce a mandate or a timeline for change, and they certainly don't preclude thoughtful, considered action. For example, when Doris came to therapy, she had been unhappy in her marriage for years. Because she was afraid to initiate change, she had tried for a long time to tell herself it wasn't that bad. Once she had a safe place to fully see and feel her unhappiness, she spent several months deliberating about what to do. When she finally came to a decision to end the marriage, we worked out a plan that took more than a year of moving in slow steps toward a separation. She took time to get used to the idea herself, to consider the timing for her two almost-grown sons, to think through and plan for her financial situation, and so on. Though the divorce was painful, Doris was well prepared both emotionally and practically for this major life change.

Blocking Belief: "If I can control, analyze, or understand my feelings with my mind, that's enough; there's no reason to actually feel them."

This belief is the collective wish of a culture with roots in Descartes's philosophy as reflected in his statement "I think, therefore I am." There are ways to engage the mind as an ally in befriending our feelings (as we'll see in the exercises that follow), but allowing the mind to dominate is not one of them. Understanding feelings can be helpful, but it is not a substitute for allowing yourself to actually feel. If we use our minds to dominate our hearts, we may feel in control, but sooner or later, we will also feel disconnected from both ourselves and others.

Naming and challenging the beliefs that contribute to our keeping difficult feelings at a distance helps to clear a path for learning to trust that we can handle whatever we find inside ourselves. If one or more of the beliefs listed earlier are blocking your path, take some time to compose an alternative belief that opens the way. For example, if you are affected by the belief that understanding or controlling your feelings rather than feeling them is enough, an alternative might be "I value both my mind and my heart" or "I receive valuable information and energy from both my feelings and my mind."

A general belief that could replace any of the blocking beliefs listed earlier is something like, "I can open, at my own pace, to what my feelings (or name a specific feeling) have to teach me (show me, give me)." Feel free to use some version of this or to create your own alternative belief with words that are right for you. When you are ready, the next step is to practice befriending a feeling.

⁊⁊⁊ Exercise: Breathing to Befriend

One of the simplest, most available aids to befriending feelings is conscious breathing. Bringing awareness to breathing can soothe discomfort or pain and help us go toward a difficult feeling rather than resist the feeling, which often intensifies it.

Because physical sensations are often easier to identify than emotions, this exercise focuses on a sensation in the body. The process of breathing to befriend is the same whether the feeling is a physical or an emotional one, so focusing on physical feelings will allow you to practice.

After you read through this exercise, close your eyes and bring your attention to your body. Scan through your body and become aware of any places of discomfort or pain. If you notice more than one uncomfortable body sensation, choose one to focus on for now. If you are not aware of any discomfort, read through the exercise now, and try it out the next time you notice physical discomfort or pain.

1. Allow your attention to move to the uncomfortable place in your body. Notice the physical sensation, and bring your awareness to the place of discomfort. Imagine that you are breathing into and all around the place that hurts. Your awareness is at once with the physical sensation and with the breath. You are not trying to make anything in particular happen. You are just breathing with the uncomfortable sensation.

2. Do this "breathing with" for a few moments, and observe your experience of the pain or discomfort. Does it change? Does your relationship to it change? Take all the time you need, then open your eyes and make some notes if you wish.

Learning to breathe with discomfort is a valuable skill in the process of befriending feelings. The next exercise takes this process another step, making use of your ability to breathe with a feeling.

☙ Exercise: Practice Befriending a Feeling

Both parts of this exercise are ways to practice befriending feelings. The first is for you to do when you're *not* in the heat of the moment, while the second is for you to use on the spot when a feeling arises unbidden in the midst of your day. In both cases, remember that the purpose of this practice is to invite more richness into your daily life. Contact with the source of that richness, the Deep River within, includes touching emotional heights and depths. When we befriend our feelings, we are cultivating the kind of emotional hardiness and resilience that allows us to be more fully alive in ourselves and more present with others.

Part 1: Going Toward a Difficult Feeling

Find a quiet spot at a time when you will be undisturbed for ten to twenty minutes. If you want, this can be your time-in for the day. Read through the exercise first; then close your eyes, opening them to read along with the steps as needed.

1. Take a couple of deep breaths, and allow your awareness to move inward. Now, *recall a situation in the recent past that evoked mildly difficult or uncomfortable feelings*. Don't choose a major fight with a loved one, a very upsetting incident at work, or the hardest time you've had in the last year. Again,

apply the principle of small steps here, choosing something relatively easy to work with—for example, being stuck in traffic, waiting for someone who was late to meet you, reading an obituary or a sad news story, or noticing a mild but unfamiliar physical sensation or symptom.

2. Once you have chosen a situation, go back to it and relive it as best as you can. In your imagination, slow down the experience or the sequence of events, and ask yourself, *"What am I feeling?"* See if you can name the emotion or emotions that are present for you in this situation. What do you feel? Anger? Frustration? Resentment? Sadness? Anxiety? Fear? Panic? Disgust? Shame? Guilt? Despair? Is there a combination of two or more feelings? If so, for the purposes of this exercise, choose whichever feeling is the deepest or strongest, most prominent one in your experience.

3. *Notice any thoughts* you may have in response to this feeling. Thoughts *about* a feeling are not the same as the raw energy of the feeling itself. This step is a chance to become conscious of the thoughts or stories we tell ourselves about what we are feeling. Take your time to become aware of the thoughts that go along with the feeling. For example, if the feeling you have identified is anger, you might have one or more of these kinds of thoughts:

   - "Here I go again, always getting upset over little things."
   - "I *hate* being angry. It's such an ugly feeling."
   - "This anger feels so good. Why don't I let myself feel this more often?"
   - "Of course I got angry. Anyone would be angry at what he did to me!"

   With an attitude of curiosity and nonjudgmental awareness, just notice and get familiar with the story line that accompanies the feeling. You can call this "story line" or "thoughts about anger." Labeling in this neutral way, without specific content, encourages an objective, observing attitude toward what we think when we feel. This nonjudgmental, witnessing attitude helps to free us from being mired in reactive thoughts about our feelings.

4. Now turn your attention to your body. Ask yourself, *"How do I experience this* _____ (name the feeling you have identified) *in my body?"* For example, do you notice
   - Shallowness or tightness in your breathing?
   - Clenching or tightness in your hands, chest, or shoulders? Your jaw? Your stomach?
   - Hollowness in the gut?
   - Shaking or tingling in your arms or legs?
   - Heat or cold in some part or all of your body?
   - Numbness or deadness in some part or all of your body?

   These are just a few possibilities. Bring your awareness to your body, and try to listen to it and observe it. Again, as best you can, be curious and try to notice body sensations with a non-judgmental awareness, not trying to change them, but simply noticing. You can name these sensations as you notice them—for example, "Tightness. Heat. Shakiness."

5. Staying with the sensation of this feeling in your body as best you can, *let it be, allow it, give it space, breathe with it.* These are all different ways of making friends with the feeling. Breathing with or breathing into the body sensations that accompany the feeling can help evoke an accepting, spacious attitude. Don't try to make the feeling change or go away. Just allow it, and get to know it. As you do this, notice what happens. Does the feeling intensify? Dissipate? Stay the same?

6. As you allow and breathe with the feeling, you can also *let a sentence or gesture or image come* that expresses the attitude of befriending this feeling. For example, if the feeling is fear, you can *say* to yourself, "I can allow fear in my experience" or "This is what fear feels like" or "I can breathe with fear" or simply "Hello, fear." A *gesture* of befriending fear might be wrapping your arms around yourself or stroking yourself in a soothing

way. An *image* of befriending fear might be a mother bear sheltering her cub.

Take whatever time you need to stay with what you're noticing as you do this, and when you're ready, open your eyes and make some notes if you want to.

This may sound like a long, complex process as you read it, but once you are familiar with the steps, moving through them usually only takes a few moments. If it helps, you can use this shorthand to remember the steps:

- Notice and name.
- Breathe and befriend.

You can adapt the process in any way that works for you. You don't need to belabor the steps or go through each one exactly. Remember that the essence of this practice is to notice, go toward, and allow yourself to experience feelings that you normally might block or move away from.

Part 2: Befriending Feelings in the Moment

In this part of the exercise, you will develop the skill of befriending feelings on the "front lines." For example, you hear that there may be major layoffs in your company, and you suddenly feel very tired and sick to your stomach. Or you discover that your partner has paid the mortgage late *again*, accruing a late fee *again*, and you feel like dropping everything and interrupting him at work to scream at him. Or you have some unexpected free time, and even though you've been wishing for this kind of time, you feel a kind of restless, vague discomfort that makes you want to fill up the time with busywork.

These are all situations with built-in opportunities to practice befriending feelings. Sometimes we know just what we are feeling, and sometimes we are so quick to move away from feelings that we don't even know that we are having an emotional response to a situation. In either case, you can practice befriending the feeling when it arises. If you immediately recognize that you are, say, angry, then you can move right to steps 3–6 in Part 1. If your emotional response is more unclear or disguised (for example, feeling tired and sick to your stomach), you can begin with noticing and naming the feeling, asking yourself, "What am I feeling right now?" (step 2 in Part 1), and then continue with steps 3–6. If you can't pause in the midst of the situation to work with befriending the feeling, then find a time and place later when you can.

––––––––––––

Practice really does result in developing a friendlier relationship with feelings. It gets easier the more you practice. Every step, no matter how small, counts as a victory. If you are able to stay with that restless discomfort even a few moments longer than you previously would have before jumping into activity, count that as a victory and record it in your victory log. If you are unable to stay with the feeling any longer, but you are more aware of the moment that you choose to jump away from it, count that as a victory and record it in your victory log.

The emotional resilience that develops as we befriend our feelings affects both our inner and our outer life. It becomes easier to take time-in and explore inner landscapes if we don't dread what we might find when we still ourselves. The more we can trust and allow our feelings as part of who we are, the more open we become to the Deep River realm and to the riches it has to offer. Outwardly, befriending our emotions has positive implications for our relationships. As we saw with both Jenna and Alice earlier in this chapter, the benefits to relationships with others are actually an outgrowth of an improved relationship with ourselves. Toward the end of her work with me, Jenna noticed that she was much more able to listen to her husband and be attentive to how he was feeling, which was clearly positive for him but also very satisfying for her. As she put it: "Once you start to have compassion for yourself, it's remarkable how much compassion you can have toward others as well!"

Chapter Seven

Tame Self-Expectations

Maybe the most important teaching is to lighten
up and relax. It's such a huge help in working with
our crazy mixed-up minds to remember that what
we're doing is unlocking a softness that is in us and
letting it spread. We're letting it blur the sharp
corners of self-criticism and complaint.
—*Pema Chödrön,* When Things Fall Apart

Although it was probably ten years ago, I still remember vividly an image shared by a woman in a Deep River group whose life was feeling unmanageable. She said she was bothered that her daily life seemed to her like a quilt with random squares missing, especially at the edges. She wanted her life to look like the quilts she made for a hobby: no missing squares, beautifully designed, everything lined up and symmetrical.

We may not all carry such a clear image of how we want our lives to look, but most of us, whether we're aware of it or not, are measuring ourselves and our lives according to some picture we have of "how it's supposed to be." These idealized images, standards, or expectations can be helpful in defining and reaching our goals, gaining skills and mastery in our chosen endeavors, and making choices that match our values. But expectations can also get us into trouble. When our expectations are too high or are held too tightly, the resulting pressure can cause us to feel driven, fragmented, and cut off from ourselves and others, not to mention unhappy. This is not an atmosphere that invites the Deep River to flow into our lives! Instead, when we have too many expectations of who we should be or what we should do, we chain ourselves to the treadmill of endless striving and doing. By lightening up on demands we put on ourselves, we not only allow for a more flexible, creative approach to life, but we begin to create an inner environment that is more friendly toward balance, depth, and ease. This receptive environment in turn makes room for contact with the Deep River within.

In Chapters Four and Five, we looked at some of the external shifts we can make to invite Deep River contact: creating time for the centering solitude of time-in and making boundaries to be sure we have time for what matters most. In Chapter Six, in examining the practice of befriending feelings, we began to look at the *internal* shifts that support the Deep River process. In this chapter, we look at learning to tame self-expectations, both about who we are and about what we do, which is another important inner skill.

Admittedly, taming self-expectations is not easy to do. Have you ever had someone tell you to "just" lighten up, and instead of helping you to lighten up, it made you furious? If we could "just do it" when it comes to being easier on ourselves, we probably would.

Life, however, has a way of teaching us to lighten up, and we may ease up on certain expectations naturally as we grow older. But there are also four proactive steps we can take to help us let go of too many "shoulds":

- Get to know the roots of expectations.
- Get to know the internal voices that maintain our expectations.
- Question those voices, and make conscious choices about lightening up.
- Find and cultivate the voice of unconditional friendliness toward ourselves.

Working with these steps is not a linear process, and you don't necessarily need to do them all to tame self-expectations. In case you read the steps above as a list of things to hurry up and do, let me remind you, as I often remind myself, that taming self-expectations is a *gradual* process, to be taken one step at a time. The first step is simply to relax and read on.

The Roots of Our Expectations

One of my favorite depictions of the roots of our expectations is a cartoon by Cathy Guisewite. Cathy is madly dusting and sweeping before guests arrive. She asks her boyfriend Irving, with a look of desperation, to help her clean all the dirt. "What dirt?" he says. She replies that the house is filthy, but Irving can't see the problem and tells her that nobody will see a little dirt. Cathy, still panicked, responds that of course the *women* will see the dirt. Irving is all rationality and says the women are as busy as she is and won't care about a little dirt. Cathy replies, "I didn't say they'll care. I said they'll notice! They'll notice because their mothers would notice! We all notice because our mothers would notice. To notice is to judge! To judge is to be criticized by a descendant of a mother I'm not even related to!! Any woman who walks through that door is a member of the universal mother force and THIS HOUSE IS FILTHY!!!" The next frame shows two couples walking in. One of the men apologizes for being late, saying his wife had to clean the oven "in case we all somehow wind up at our house and someone wants to bake something." The other man says, "Linda had to iron the drapes." And Irving replies, "No rush. Cathy's re-papering all the drawers in the bathroom."[1]

In addition to having a sense of humor about the ways that our standards can make us a bit crazy, a first step in freeing ourselves from overly high expectations is to take a good look at where they come from. Our individual history, shaped by parents and other family members' traditions, values, and beliefs, has helped to create the standards we hold for ourselves. If mom—and perhaps her mom before her—believed in *always* bathing before bed, then skipping a night may elicit a range of reactions inside, from a twinge of guilt and anxiety to a sense of wild rebellion or shameful transgression. If there was no one set time or method for getting clean in your family, that might sound a little crazy. But the standards we adopt unconsciously in childhood can be very powerful.

I have a friend whose mother always baked desserts from scratch because that was the one and only right way to do it. In her twenties, my friend exhausted herself by having a retirement party for a beloved professor who taught in her graduate program. She baked eight desserts from scratch, not because she particularly enjoyed baking, but because she couldn't *not* do it according to the expectation she had inherited. Not only did she need a full day of recuperation after her baking marathon, but she had been so focused on producing and presenting the desserts that she didn't enjoy the party.

In addition to the do's and don'ts instilled by our upbringing, we are all affected at least to some degree by the collective standards of our culture. Whether we adopt or reject them, we have to contend with their influence. These include norms for what we are supposed to look like physically and what level of health and physical ability we should have. Sometimes they're contradictory, as in the expectation that we should be independent but also be capable of attracting a partner or be partnered. Norms can accumulate to such an extent that they feel crushing: we should be a competent member of the workforce and an active participant in the community, as well as an attentive, organized, and caring mother, or both. In essence, our society fosters the ideal of being Superwoman. This standard rewards keeping busy, endlessly multitasking, and generally being all things to all people at all times (while looking beautiful).

Also part of "the water we swim in" are the culturewide expectations connected to what is commonly called "the American dream." This ideal, now exported well beyond the borders of the United States, is based on expectations of bettering oneself economically, physically, and educationally. Add to that the never-ending American quest for self-improvement that has become particularly strong in the last thirty years, and we now have such a vast array of possibilities for improving ourselves that *not* doing so at every turn and in every aspect of our lives can seem downright lazy. When these "opportunities" for improvement are offered in the context of a culture that values achievement and doing rather than being, the pressure to achieve perfection, as impossible a goal as that is, can be enormous.

Internal Voices

The "Blocking Belief" section of Chapter Five describes how our personalities are made up of multiple parts. We can see the workings of these parts of our personalities in our lives through the ways we behave and the ways we talk to ourselves. Recognizing two of these internal voices—the voice of perfectionism and the voice of the inner critic—and understanding how they work can play a major role in our efforts to tame self-expectations.

The Voice of Perfectionism

The external norms of our culture magnify and are magnified by the internal voice of perfectionism, which urges us to do it right, do it all, and never make a mistake. Whether that voice originates in efforts to live up to family expectations or the cultural ideal of Superwoman or both, this is the part within us that expects life—and ourselves—to be like a perfectly finished quilt: no missing pieces, no loose ends, no rough edges. In her book *Bird by Bird*, writer Anne Lamott does not mince words about the effects of perfectionism on writing and on life: "Perfectionism is the voice of the oppressor, the enemy of the people. It will keep you cramped and insane your whole life. . . . Perfectionism will ruin your writing, blocking inventiveness and playfulness and life force. . . . Perfectionism means that you try desperately not to leave so much mess to clean up. But clutter and mess show us that life is being lived. Clutter is wonderfully fertile ground. . . . Tidiness makes me think of held breath, of suspended animation, while writing needs to breathe and move."[2]

Perfectionism, whether it manifests in creative endeavors like writing or in how we relate to ourselves and live our lives, has a tendency to freeze or deaden the otherwise free-flowing energy of life. In her book *Addiction to Perfection*, Jungian psychologist Marion

Woodman describes an extreme example of a young woman caught in the grip of perfectionism:

> Eleanor . . . was a pillar of strength in school and in the community. Throughout her life she had been an outstanding student, a good athlete and a good leader. At twenty-three she found herself eating nothing but popcorn, unable to make decisions, unable to speak to anyone. . . . When she could no longer handle her work efficiently, she had to go into the hospital. . . . After some weeks she had the confidence to show me her book of lists—yearly lists, monthly lists, weekly lists, daily lists, special daily lists—all meticulously organized.
>
> When I suggested that there had to be room for some spontaneity, she dutifully agreed. But a week later, she sadly assured me, "There's no point in making time for spontaneity, there simply isn't any in my life." And later in the session when I looked at her daily list I saw: "2:15–2:30p.m.—Spontaneity." In that simple sentence lay the tragedy of her life.[3]

While Eleanor's internal voice commanding her to be perfect is especially severe, many women are drawn toward the mirage of perfection. In my twenties, I had a dream that to me captures the power and lure of perfectionism. In the dream, a girl is walking barefoot on a path down a mountain. She has lived on the top of the mountain until now. The air is pure and clear at the top, and she can see smog and feel the thicker air as she descends. She keeps walking downward, but she yearns to be back in the pure air of the mountaintop and feels inconsolably sad.

I realized, with the help of the dream, that in many ways, in my life up until that time, I had been trying to keep myself pure and at a distance from life, especially from the messy, earthy, dirty imperfection of it. Although I didn't know how to go about it then, I recognized that this dream was about letting go of perfectionism. I did feel very sad having to leave that pure air, and the journey down the mountain has taken many more years than I imagined back then. But I understand now not only that there is joy and freedom in accepting imperfection but also that the girl had to come down the mountain to truly enter into life and grow up. I also understand now that she (I) had to make the descent in order to find the Deep River.

Unlike the airy spirituality of the mountaintop, the Deep River is home to a spirituality that is embodied and flowing with life. Although we may have to remove ourselves from the busyness of the world to connect with it, it does not reject the world but rather helps us engage more deeply *in* the world. The Deep River realm embraces a stillness that is vital and alive, not the quiet deadness of perfection. Anne Lamott expresses this kind of grounded spirituality in her writings about faith: "Holiness has most often been revealed to me in the exquisite pun of the first syllable, in holes— in not enough help, in brokenness, mess. High holy places, with ethereal sounds and stained glass, can massage my illusion of holiness, but in holes and lostness I can pick up the light of small ordinary progress."[4] Touching the Deep River can help us open to compassionate acceptance of ourselves and this world we live in, brokenness and all.

The Inner Critic—That Old Familiar Voice

If the voice of perfectionism sets the bar for what we expect of ourselves, the inner critic is the voice that measures our progress. These two parts of ourselves are close cousins—for some of us, they may be one and the same. Julia Cameron calls the inner critic "the Censor"[5]; Clarissa Estés calls it "the Harpy" and its messages "Harpy-talk."[6] (In Greek mythology, harpies are the fierce vulture-like birds that steal food from their victims, leaving them only enough to survive.) Marion Woodman calls the inner critic "the black crow sitting on my left shoulder."[7] Some call it the Judge because its self-assigned job seems to be to compare and judge us in just about every arena. The inner critic has an uncanny ability to shoot us down and make us doubt ourselves and feel inadequate.

In my own life, the voice of the inner critic arrived early and has been tenacious. In grade school, my inner critic focused primarily on making sure I did well in school. For several years in elementary

school, I got headaches every Monday morning, which I later cred-
ited to pressure from my budding young inner critic. In middle
school and high school, its domain expanded to include body image,
popularity, and ability (or lack thereof) to attract boys. According
to my inner critic, I weighed too much and was too tall, my nose was
too big, my breasts too small. I remember looking at my arms in the
middle school cafeteria one day and thinking they were too hairy.
I know I was mortified at the time, but I still can't figure out how I
drew that conclusion from what I saw.

In college in the late 1960s, hair was in, so my arms were no
longer an issue, but judgment about academic achievement and physical attractiveness continued. In addition, my inner critic took up two
new causes: now I was being judged on my creativity and my spirituality. In my sophomore year, a professor assigned a paper for a sociol-
ogy course and said we could write it about any topic we chose. Well,
having that much freedom brought out my inner critic in spades.
Every time I had an idea, the Harpy-talk began. "That's a stupid idea!"
"What? You want to write about *that?*" "It's been done, and much better than you could ever do it. Don't you have any *original* ideas?" And
on and on. I was absolutely paralyzed. I finally wrote a paper about
how hard it was for me to write a paper with no assigned topic.

In college, I began a practice of yoga and meditation, and my
inner critic had a heyday. There were always plenty of more accomplished yogis to compare myself with, and in meditation, my inner
critic piped up every time I realized that my mind was wandering.
With full enlightenment (whatever I thought that was at the time)
as the ultimate goal, my inner critic had no shortage of evidence of
how I wasn't measuring up.

And so it went. My inner critic accompanied me and found ways
to insert itself into most anything I undertook: first job, graduate
school, marriage, motherhood, community participation, home-
maker. I would love to be able to describe next some amazing trans-
formative moment when my inner critic suddenly rose up into the
sky and disappeared in a cloud of smoke, never to whisper—or yell—
in my ear again. All I can say is, here I am writing a book, and during

the process, that old familiar voice has certainly let me know that it hasn't deserted me entirely!

Questioning Our Expectations

When the internal voices of perfectionism and the inner critic join with family norms and the cultural ideal of Superwoman to shape our self-expectations, the combination can be overwhelming—or worse. It's no wonder that we feel driven to be and do more and anxious about not measuring up. To relieve some of the pressure, we can begin to question the sources of our expectations and see whether they match our true, current priorities. This kind of examination makes it easier to exercise some choice about the standards we hold for ourselves.

Who Says?

One simple way to question our self-expectations is by asking, "Who says?" Who says the beds must be made before I go to work (go for a walk, write in my journal, meet a friend)? Asking, "Who says?" might yield some understanding of where in your history this particular "should" originated. Or it might be more of a rhetorical question that means, "Is there some kind of rule that says I *have* to make beds before anything else happens?" In either case, the question creates a pause so that you can remember that you have a choice. It gives you space to ask yourself, "Is this really important to *me*? Even if this *was* important to me at one time in my life, is it important to me *now*?" The answer might be "Yes. My mother taught me how to make my bed when I was eight. It was my way of making order in my life as a child, and it gives me satisfaction, pleasure, and a sense of order now as I start my day." If this is so, then bed making is a ritual to keep right where it is. But let's say that you are in the habit of making beds in the morning and your answer about its importance is "No, I actually don't care whether my bed is made early, later, or not at all. My mother liked everything neat and orderly, but a little chaos doesn't bother me. In fact, I find rumpled sheets cozy and inviting. I can think of a hundred things I would rather do before making beds." If this is true for you, then it might be time to let go of daily bed making and reprioritize your morning routine.

Recognizing the possibility of choice is important. Carol, a Deep River group participant, explains:

> Realizing that I *have* choices is an awakening unto itself. It is so easy for me to slip into the mode where my self-expectations rule the day. When I can, I check myself. I ask, "Who says I must do *x*, *y*, or *z*? Do I want to? Does it have to be done by a certain date, or in a certain way, or am I just doing it to calm myself?" In fact, my self-expectations are often driven by fear. Here's how the inner dialogue goes: "If I don't prepare like crazy for my teaching job next fall, I will fail. Wait a minute—who says I am so underprepared? I do, no one else. OK, now I can start to let go and focus on what actually needs to get done, so that the rest of the summer is mine free and clear." I've learned that I can question the expectations; I don't need to be a slave to them.

Lightening Up

The purpose of working with our self-expectations is not to eradicate them altogether but simply to lighten up a bit, as Buddhist teacher Pema Chödrön suggests. One way to do that is to experiment with how you hold your expectations in your mind—that is, your mental standards for how you are supposed to be or behave. For example, you may have a standard of an immaculate home in your mind yet often have a fairly messy house. The issue here is not whether or not you live up to this standard; it is the standard itself. If you hold tightly to the expectation of a clean, orderly home, when there is disorder, your stress increases, not because the house is messy but because of the *gap* between how it is and how you think it should be. With the same amount of disorder and a more lightly held expectation, you have less stress. A lighter expectation might sound like this: "I'd like it to be clean, but it doesn't *have* to be clean *all* the time." This mental shift makes it possible to befriend chaos if need be. At the risk of stating the obvious, none of us can live without some mess. If we want to actually *live* in our homes rather than trying futilely to make them perfect, it helps to make friends with disorder. Otherwise, we may drive ourselves crazy in trying to avoid it and beat up on ourselves when disorder inevitably happens.

When we hold ourselves rigidly or tightly to an expectation, we *believe* (whether it's objectively true or not) that whatever needs to be done must be done *now* (that is, it's urgent!), *perfectly* (that is, no cutting corners!), and *just so* (that is, no flexibility about how, whether, or when it gets done). Can you feel, in just imagining trying to do things this way, that it's a little hard to breathe? That's why learning to hold an expectation more loosely can allow us more breathing room.

Loosening up takes away the life-or-death urgency we sometimes assign to things that really aren't matters of life or death. It means accepting that we have limitations and developing a greater tolerance for imperfection and for the inevitable loose ends in ourselves and in our lives. It means giving ourselves a break.

When you think of holding an expectation more lightly, what comes to mind? For some women, it might mean, "I'd love to have time to make a Batman costume, but maybe I'll still be a good person if I don't make my child's Halloween costume this year (or ever!)." Or "I know my in-laws (and I) like a clean kitchen, but maybe my world won't come to an end if I don't get the oven cleaned before they arrive." Or "Today is a designated exercise day, but given the rough night I had last night, maybe I won't turn into a couch potato forevermore if I don't exercise today." Or "Maybe a year from now it won't matter that I returned this phone call tomorrow (or next week!) instead of today."

Of course, some phone calls require immediate attention, and we may choose not to compromise on certain expectations. But to bring our lives into balance, we need to find the places where we can lighten up on our expectations and give ourselves permission to relax a little. In my own life and in my work with countless women over the years, I have seen a great deal of physical, emotional, and mental energy go into needless striving toward perfection in situations that, seen with even a little bit of perspective, don't really matter that much.

For my friend who gave the dessert party in her twenties, her experience that night was the beginning of a gradual process of lightening up on her expectations about making everything from scratch. She began to accept that elaborate cooking was an enjoyable pastime for her mother, but not for her. At first, she felt guilty buying cake mixes or bakery-made desserts. But now, in her forties, she is clear that her worth as a person is entirely separate from whether she bakes, buys, or otherwise obtains a dessert when it's called for. This lighter attitude has enabled her to enjoy baking a cake from scratch now and then with her own children. She says, "The point of it for me is to create something with my children and have fun doing it. I know they're learning things in the process, but the emphasis is not on 'This is how it *should* be done and how one must *always* do it.'"

Taking Things as They Are

The ability to lighten up on expectations rests on a worldview that definitely does *not* belong to the critical, judgmental part within us. In my case, since my early twenties, I had held a strong assumption, germinated in the soil of an opportunity-rich upper-middle-class postwar upbringing and nourished by the human potential movement: I believed that we human beings had limitless potential to grow, transform, and achieve whatever we might imagine. This belief that we could become anything we set out to be, while in some ways exhilarating, gave my inner critic a foothold in every aspect of my life that had room for improvement. "How I was" always seemed to compare unfavorably with "how I *could* be."

But in my early forties, something started to shift. I began to question the assumption of endless possibility. Now definitively past my youth, it occurred to me that while in theory I had endless potential for growth, in actuality some of my traits, habits, fears, and stuck places might never change. I began to listen with new ears to all the readings and teachings in both psychology and spirituality about accepting myself and taking things as they are. I pondered Pema Chödrön's words, "Our wisdom is all mixed up with what we call our neurosis. Our brilliance, our juiciness, our spiciness, is all mixed up with our craziness and our confusion, and therefore it doesn't do any good to try to get rid of our so-called negative aspects, because in that process we also get rid of our basic wonderfulness."[8] I thought about Lucy in *I Love Lucy*—how lovable and imperfect she was and how her juiciness and spiciness were truly all mixed up with her craziness and confusion. As a way to accept the whole package of "me," I tried to picture myself as a character on a sitcom, full of endearing foibles like Lucy.

This kind of thinking was gravely threatening to my inner critic. But despite the protests of that old familiar voice, the softer voice of self-acceptance did begin to emerge and, gradually, in Pema Chödrön's words, "blur the sharp corners of self-criticism and complaint." From a more accepting perspective, I could see that maybe the key to happiness was to come into a *new relationship* with my issues rather than try to fix myself and be done with them.

The Gentle Power of Acceptance

My work as a therapist has made it abundantly clear that I'm not the only one with an overactive critic. I don't think it is too big a generalization to say that we, men and women alike, are much more proficient at self-criticism than self-acceptance. In this culture, the idea that we might not *always* be trying to "get rid of our so-called negative aspects" is a radical way of thinking. As a culture, we gravitate much more toward "fix it, make it go away" than toward "accept it, let it be."

Part of the process of slowing down and creating balance and depth in our lives involves learning how to let ourselves be and to accept things as they are. This is the same attitude of unconditional friendliness or deep acceptance that I spoke of in Chapter Six. We can cultivate such an attitude not only in befriending difficult feelings but also in accepting ourselves in all of our strengths and weaknesses, in all of who we are and what we do.

I think of this kind of acceptance as an altered state of awareness, because when I experience it, I realize how radically different it is from my usual state of mind. Ordinarily, my inner critic carries on a running commentary in the back of my mind, and there is a subtle quality of trying or of pushing against life that I don't even notice except in contrast to this more open state of mind. When I am able to let go, even briefly, of how I want things to be or how I wish they could be or how I expect them to be and surrender to how things *actually are*, I find that I am released from judging commentary and needless effort. Sometimes the voice of my inner critic is silenced, and sometimes it is still audible, but it doesn't dominate. It is as if the critical part of me gets smaller—or *seems* smaller—in the spaciousness that is created when I accept myself compassionately. Meditation teacher Sharon Salzburg explains the space-giving effect of what she calls "the vast transforming field of acceptance" with the analogy of the difference between putting a teaspoon of salt into a small glass of water and putting that same amount into a large body of water such as a lake. The amount of salt is the same; the impact of it changes entirely due to the vastness of the container receiving it.[9] Loving acceptance has the effect of enlarging the container of what we can allow in ourselves and receive in our lives. We hear the inner critic's salty comments, yet somehow they are effortlessly dissolved in the lake of loving kindness created by self-acceptance.

The idea of deeply, unconditionally accepting all of who we are is, for most of us, at once an extremely alluring possibility and a seemingly impossible goal. The truth is, it isn't easy to cultivate self-acceptance, but it can be done. I have been helped the most in this process by Buddhist teachings, which contain methods developed many centuries ago and used by millions of people to help minds and hearts incline toward unconditional friendliness, which in Buddhism is called *metta* or *maitri*. The Selected Reading at the end of this book lists some good resources for learning more about these methods and ideas.

Acceptance and Change

Self-acceptance is hard to cultivate because the judgmental part of ourselves can grab onto just about anything, even judging us for not lightening up or not slowing down enough or not doing the practices in this book enough. When the inner critic gets hold of the Deep River process, the net result is more stress about how to get unstressed, business as usual for the inner critic, and not much peace.

The wonderful paradox of acceptance has been aptly described by psychologist Carl Rogers, who said, "When I accept myself just as I am, then I can change."[10] We tend to assume that if we accept something about ourselves, it will become even more entrenched and we'll be stuck with it forever. So we think that if we distance ourselves from whatever we consider to be a negative pattern or trait, that will make it go away. As we saw in working with difficult feelings in Chapter Six, this is not usually an effective strategy. I described Jenna's experience of trying to keep her fear at a distance for years. She had started therapy because this strategy wasn't working. When she accepted the fear—that is, when she changed her relationship to it rather than trying to make it go away—it became much more manageable and her actions were no longer determined by it.

There are two aspects of acceptance as the ground for change. First, acceptance allows us to see clearly, acknowledge, and perhaps understand more fully what we are dealing with. For example, in Chapter Six, Alice had been angry about her brother's infidelity. When she shifted from trying to push down her anger to allowing and paying close attention to it, she contacted the sadness beneath it and gained a much clearer understanding of what the anger was about. For Alice, the process of turning toward and accepting her anger allowed it to dissipate spontaneously. Acceptance may not always work so smoothly, but since true acceptance often does lead to change, it's easy to begin trying to "accept" something as a tricky means of getting it to go away! This usually doesn't work, because true acceptance involves the other key ingredient of acceptance as the ground for change: the quality of kindness or compassion. It means creating that "bigger container" in our minds and hearts, which can shift our perspective and our relationship to whatever we are experiencing from one of struggle to one of letting it be.

For example, Clare is a client who struggles with insomnia. We have worked to improve her sleep habits and implement various relaxation techniques, with moderate success. Recently, Clare had an experience that gave her a new way of approaching her wakefulness:

> I was lying awake, trying to relax, trying to stop my "worry thoughts," trying to get comfortable but also trying to be less restless and not move so much. And I was berating myself for not being able to relax; how relaxing was *that*? After this had gone on for a while, somehow I stepped back in my mind and became aware of all the *trying*. I could see myself as this struggling person who was trying *so hard* to get some rest, and I felt compassion for myself. In that softer frame of mind, I had this thought: "It's fine to be awake. It's really OK. I'm OK." This is what is so amazing—it *really* was OK with me to be awake! And wouldn't you know it, with all the tension gone, I lay there for a while, and then I fell asleep.

The "pushing" or "trying" or critical part of us may sometimes be a spur to change, but often the change doesn't last because we are resisting or fighting ourselves in the process. Sooner or later, we rebel. The inner critic, for example, might get us to diet, but eventually other parts of ourselves get fed up with dietary constraints, and the "yo-yo effect" begins. Acceptance of habits that are harmful to ourselves or others can seem like the very opposite of what we should do. Pema Chödrön explains, "Trying to fix ourselves is not helpful. It implies struggle and self-denigration. . . . [But] does not trying to change mean we have to remain angry and addicted until the day we die? This is a reasonable question. Trying to change ourselves doesn't work in the long run because we're resisting our own energy. Self-improvement can have temporary results, but . . . only when we relate with ourselves without moralizing, without harshness, without deception, can we let go of harmful patterns."[11]

I have found that cultivating this way of relating to myself—with unconditional friendliness—continues to be one of the most challenging and important aspects of the inner journey. I paraphrase here Pema Chödrön's frequent reminder about having patience in this process; her words give me perspective as I travel slightly different versions of this same path year after year. "And how long do we have to practice this? How long does it take?" she asks. The answer? "The rest of our lives."[12]

> The bud
> stands for all things,
> even for those things that don't flower,
> for everything flowers, from within, of self-blessing;
> though sometimes it is necessary
> to reteach a thing its loveliness,
> to put a hand on the brow
> of the flower
> and retell it in words and in touch
> it is lovely
> until it flowers again from within, of self-blessing;
> as Saint Francis
> put his hand on the creased forehead
> of the sow, and told her in words and in touch
> blessings of earth on the sow, and the sow
> began remembering all down her thick length,
> from the earthen snout all the way
> through the fodder and slops to the spiritual curl of the tail,
> from the hard spininess spiked out from the spine
> down through the great broken heart
> to the sheer blue milken dreaminess spurting and shuddering

from the fourteen teats into the fourteen mouths sucking and
blowing beneath them:
the long, perfect loveliness of sow.

—Galway Kinnell, *Saint Francis and the Sow*

Blocking Belief: "I have to be a certain way." "It has to be done a certain way."

The most common core belief that keeps us stuck in our expectations about *who we are* is, essentially, "I have to be a certain way." The blocking belief that pertains to expectations about *what we do* is, essentially, "It has to be done a certain way." Because taming self-expectations involves a shift of mental attitude, when we can move past these blocking beliefs, that movement in itself is a loosening of tightly held expectations. For example, if I let go of the assumption that I have to write this paragraph one certain way, that mental shift allows me to consider many other options. Sometimes, to tame expectations, we only need permission not to be or do things a certain way and some suggestions about how to let go. Here, I offer a few ways to identify expectations in the midst of your day, then a list of possible ways to make a mental shift toward lightening up.

A Few Ways to Identify Expectations

- *Look for inner "shoulds" or "judge" or "critic" energy:* "I should have returned that phone call yesterday."

  This type of expectation can come with or without the accompanying self-defeating commentary—for example, "I *always* procrastinate on returning phone calls; I'm so disorganized (selfish, lazy, _____ [fill in the blank])."

- *Look for urgency:* "I *have* to return this phone call *now* or else _____ (fill in the blank)."

- *Look for rigidity:* "I'm returning the phone call now because I *always* return phone calls immediately, so no, I *can't* go out to lunch with you on the spur of the moment, even though it would be fun and nurturing" or "I can't _____ (fill in the blank)."

- *Look for conflict with others:* This is similar to the preceding item on rigidity. You might be holding to your expectation so tightly that you can't see anyone else's point of view, can't compromise, can't consider a creative middle ground, can't _____ (fill in the blank).

- *Look for passionate justifying of anything to anyone, including yourself:* You might try to justify your sinkful of dishes to your neighbor, your nap to your spouse, your night out to your kids, or _____ (fill in the blank).

- *Listen to your body:* Get to know where and how your inner critic typically shows itself in your body (for example, tightness in the neck, shoulders, jaw, gut; shallow breathing; allergies acting up).

A Few Ways to Hold Expectations More Loosely

Holding expectations more loosely doesn't mean giving them up altogether. It means letting go of urgency, rigidity, and the need for things to be "just so" *when those qualities are not warranted.* This is a key to slowing down and having less stress in your life.

The first step in loosening up is becoming *aware* of the expectation, which we just discussed. Once you are aware of holding an expectation tightly, try some of the following suggestions for how to lighten up. You can figure out what works for you by trial and error.

- *Try humor:* Exaggerate your expectation to the point of absurdity. Make a caricature of yourself. Imagine how you would look or what you would say in a cartoon, sitcom, or comic strip. Or listen to the voice of your inner critic and identify what it is saying to you. Then, hear those words spoken to you in the voice of Donald Duck on helium.[13]

- *Try compassion:* See your self-expectation from the perspective of a very trusted and loving friend, teacher, or family member. What does this compassionate person say to you? Try saying it to yourself. Or try seeing your expectation as if it was someone else's—someone you care about. What would you say to that person? Try saying it to yourself. Or have a compassionate conversation with the part of you that is holding on so tightly. (Hint: Is this perhaps a child part of you?) Lovingly acknowledge it for *trying so hard* to be more this, less that, and so forth.

- *Try expanding time:* Ask yourself, "Will this matter ten years from now?"

- *Try expanding space:* Look, even briefly, at a star-filled night sky or the vastness of an ocean or a prairie or a clear blue sky. See if your expectation loosens.

- *Try breathing:* Feel where and how you are holding this expectation in your body. Imagine breathing into it, around it. Let your breath make space around the tightness, helping it to soften. Or just take three slow, deep breaths.

- *Try coming up with a reminder phrase that you can say to yourself:* You might tell yourself, for example, "Don't sweat the small stuff—and it's all small stuff."[14] Or you might say, "Que sera sera; whatever will be will be."[15] If you can sing your phrase, all the better! If you prefer more Buddhist phrasing, try these: "Things are as they are" or "This is what is." One that works for me when things aren't going according to plan and I start to blame myself: "Nothing is wrong here."[16] It helps me shift from trying to control life to remembering that life is as it is, and it seems to stop my inner critic cold.

- *Try telling yourself "I'll still be a good person if . . .* I don't bake my child's birthday cake from scratch" or "if I go to bed and read instead of cleaning up the kitchen" or "if I _____ (fill in the blank)." Have a friend remind you that you're still a good person even if _____ (fill in the blank) when you forget it or doubt it.

- *Try asking yourself, "Who says?"* With a little introspection, you might trace your self-expectation to someone else (Mom? Dad? The religious or other belief system you grew up with?) or simply to one of your own internal voices. Even if you can't identify the source of your expectation, asking the question provides a pause and the possibility of making a choice about how and whether to meet that expectation.

❧ Exercises to Help You Loosen Up Self-Expectations

The suggestions here and in the "Blocking Belief" section of this chapter are just that—suggestions, possibilities. My intention is to help loosen the grip of your critic, perfectionist, or judge, not to make a longer list of "shoulds" for you to do! So ask the perfectionist or critical part of yourself to step aside as you choose when and whether to try any of these exercises.

Exercise: From "Shoulds" to "Coulds"

This simple exercise can help relieve the burden of too many expectations.

1. When you're feeling weighed down by "shoulds," take a few moments with your journal or a piece of paper and make an uncensored list of them—for example,

   I should fold the laundry.

   I should work on that report today.

   I should get to the gym.

   I should change my hairstyle.

   I should be less critical.

I should drink less diet soda.

I should be more patient with Ella.

This is not a ponderous exercise. Just write down whatever "shoulds" you're aware of at the moment. They can range from practical to do's to spiritual qualities you aspire to. If you think of a "should" and have the thought "I shouldn't expect that of myself," then add that to the list: "I shouldn't expect (whatever it is) of myself." The purpose is to get your "shoulds" out of your head and onto the paper. It objectifies (and sometimes makes quite laughable) the amount of pressure we put on ourselves. If you have time, go on to the next step; if not, continue with it at another time.

2. Choose one of the "shoulds" you wrote in step 1, preferably one that you are holding rather tightly. Read the sentence to yourself, beginning with "I should." Notice what happens in your body in response to this "should." If you need to, repeat the sentence to yourself, paying attention to your physical response as you do. For example, do you notice any change in your breathing or any sensations in your gut? In your neck or shoulders? In your legs or arms?

Once you have noted your physical response, take a deep breath and relax your body. Now, repeat the same sentence, but this time, change the word *should* to *could*. For example, instead of saying "I should fold the laundry," say, "I could fold the laundry." Again, notice what happens in your body in response to this sentence. If you need to, repeat the sentence a few times, focusing your attention on your physical response. Take some time to write down your experience, if you wish.

Moving from "I should" to "I could" is a simple, direct way of shifting from pressure to choice. Once you are aware of how the pressure of your self-expectations lives in your body, you can use that awareness to identify "shoulds" in the midst of activity and to consciously shift from "shoulding" and the posture of critical pressure to "coulding" and the more accepting posture of choice.

———————————

Exercise: Wabi-Sabi Eyes

Wabi-sabi is a Japanese concept that celebrates the beauty in simple, humble things that are imperfect, incomplete, or impermanent. It is a deep thread in Japanese culture, one that our airbrushed society could learn from. Robyn Griggs Lawrence, editor of *Natural Home* magazine, describes the essence of wabi-sabi with this story: "According to Japanese legend, a young man named Sen no Rikyu sought to learn the elaborate set of customs known as the Way of Tea. He went to tea-master Takeeno Joo, who tested the younger man by asking him to tend the garden. Rikyu cleaned up debris and raked the ground until it was perfect, then scrutinized the immaculate garden. Before presenting his work to the master, he shook a cherry tree, causing a few flowers to spill randomly onto the ground."[17]

The blossoms spilled on the ground were the imperfection that, in Rikyu's eyes, enhanced the beauty of the garden. If you have noticed that you have a perfectionist streak, try a little wabi-sabi! What if you *aspired* to imperfection? Can you see the beauty in a few dirty dishes left in the sink? Your child's unbrushed hair? Lawrence says, "Wabi-sabi reminds us that we are all transient beings on this planet—that our bodies, as well as the material world around us, are in the process of returning to dust. Nature's cycles of growth, decay, and erosion are embodied in frayed edges, rust, liver spots. Through wabi-sabi, we learn to embrace both the glory and the melancholy found in these marks of passing time."[18]

Wabi-sabi is a different way of seeing, a good antidote to seeing through the eyes of perfection. Next time you want to jump up and comb that hair or wash those dishes or straighten those piles, pause for a moment and see if you can appreciate whatever it is, just as it is. Just for a moment, try seeing it through wabi-sabi eyes.

———————————

On Finding the Voice of Acceptance

I thought about including an exercise on finding the inner voice of unconditional friendliness toward yourself. In my view, this is a deeply important attitude to cultivate, not only for taming self-expectations but as a basis for our daily living, our relationships, and our growth. All of the suggestions in the "Blocking Belief" and "Exercises" sections of this chapter can help to awaken this voice of compassion. But in truth, there is no exercise I can put here that will—presto!—transform self-criticism into deep, abiding acceptance. Instead, I suggest that you notice when it happens by grace, which it sometimes does—for instance, when for no particular reason, you respond to a mistake you've made with kindness rather than criticism. In the meantime, try lots of things, use whatever works, keep in mind that each small step is a victory, and remember that the journey toward acceptance is a worthy path, worthy of traveling for the rest of your life!

> The bud
> stands for all things,
> even for those things that don't flower,
> for everything flowers, from within, of self-blessing;
> though sometimes it is necessary
> to reteach a thing its loveliness,
> to put a hand on the brow
> of the flower
> and retell it in words and in touch
> it is lovely
> until it flowers again from within, of self-blessing . . .

Chapter Eight

Practice Presence

We know how to sacrifice ten years for a diploma,
and we are willing to work very hard to get a job,
a car, a house, and so on. But we have difficulty
remembering that we are alive in the present moment, the only moment there is for us to be alive.
—*Thich Nhat Hanh,* Peace Is Every Step

Experiencing the power of presence is a little like looking at one of those holographic pictures that were popular a few years ago on calendars and posters. It appears two-dimensional, but if you look at it slightly differently, another, three-dimensional picture magically leaps into view. The other picture was right there all along, but until you looked in a particular way, you couldn't see it, even though it was right in front of your eyes.

We are always living in the present moment, which is, as Thich Nhat Hanh says, "the only moment there is for us to be alive." But when we wake up to this fact and actually *experience* being present, a different, fuller picture of what it means to be truly alive, one that was there all along, leaps into view. To get a sense of what I mean by *presence,* consider the examples that follow. As you read them, you may be reminded of experiences of your own.

- *From a Deep River group participant:* "I was in the car, the kids were in the back seat, and I was rushing to get an errand done. Then somehow I realized I was rushing, and I was able to slow down. We came to a traffic light, and I stopped the car, but also *I* stopped. And

I was just there, in an ordinary moment, but really fully *there*. And I thought to myself, 'This moment is good. This moment is rich.'"

• *From meditation teacher Jon Kabat-Zinn, in his book* Wherever You Go, There You Are: "As I pull into the parking lot of the hospital, several hundred geese pass overhead. They are flying northwest, and there are so many of them that the formation trails out far to the east, where the early November sun is hugging the horizon. . . . Hundreds are in V's, but many are in more complex arrangements. Everything is in motion. Their lines dip and ascend with grace and harmony, like a cloth waving in the air. . . .

"I feel strangely blessed by their passage. This moment is a gift. . . . My usual experience of time flowing is suspended while witnessing their passage. . . . For me it is simply the gift of wonder and amazement."[1]

• *From another Deep River group member:* "Things were pressing on me, and yet I took time to create earrings. I might have spent hours with the beads, just the feel and the colors of the beads and the process of combining them together and creating the earrings. I was *finding* myself in that activity. We tend to say we *lose* ourselves in an activity, but this was really more finding myself."

• *From meditation teacher Jane Dobisz, toward the end of a solitary hundred-day retreat described in her book* The Wisdom of Solitude: "One of the main purposes of my coming here was to get my mind and body in the same place at the same time. More than three months into this adventure, it's happening more frequently—certainly more so than when I first arrived. By making my focus smaller and smaller, everything is getting bigger and bigger. Just rinsing out the breakfast dishes, I am happy. There's a vast space around things in which anything is possible. A sense of rapture permeates even the smallest activities of the day."[2]

All of these accounts describe experiences of presence—that is, of paying attention in the present moment. Presence is, as Dobisz puts it, getting "mind and body in the same place at the same time." Or you could say that presence is actually doing what you're doing when you're doing it. Doesn't that sound simple? If you've ever spent any time noticing the workings of your mind, with its incessant chatter, innate distractibility, and frequent trips into the past and future, then you know that being present is not as easy as it sounds. In fact, Kabat-Zinn says, "To be present . . . may be the hardest work in the world. And forget about the 'may be.' It *is* the hardest work in the world—at least to sustain presence."[3]

So what does practicing presence have to do with the Deep River process? This practice is different from the other practices discussed so far. The preceding four chapters all describe tools that are means to invite Deep River access, or doorways to the Deep River realm. Presence is both a *doorway to* the Deep River and a *way of experiencing* the Deep River. It could be described as both part of the journey and part of the destination.

In order to slow down and experience life with more balance, depth, and satisfaction, we need to address both the outer and the inner dimensions of how we live. The practice of presence addresses *internal* busyness, the constant stream of mental chatter that can fill even the most spacious times our calendar has to offer. This habit of mental busyness effectively blocks us from the one place where we can experience life fully and deeply: the present moment. It is in the here and now that life really happens: we engage with what matters, open to ourselves and others, experience joy. All of these are also hallmarks of living with access to the waters of the Deep River.

When we are caught up in mental busyness and are *not* present, we stay on the surface of life. In this state, we can certainly get things done, but we tend to feel more restlessness than contentment or joy as we go through the motions of our lives. The practice of presence offers the opportunity to deepen our experience of life and enjoy it more fully moment to moment.

Meg's "before" and "after" experience of painting her deck is a good example of the difference between doing an activity in a state of restless distraction and doing an activity with presence. Meg came to one of the Deep River groups after leaving a high-powered, high-stress job and was, for the time being, unemployed. She had become fully acclimated to speeding across the surface of life, and practicing presence did not figure much into her scheme of things. Because she was finally spending more time at home than just quick pit stops, Meg noticed that the deck railing needed painting. She also noticed that the deck had a *lot* of spindles. She thought, "Well, how hard could that be?" and she bought what she needed to do the job.

She began, but then found the task more difficult than she had thought it would be. "It wasn't hard in the sense of not having enough painting skill," she reported. "It was just so hard to slow myself down—physically, but especially mentally—to *stand* the pace of that. It was torture! I struggled through the process every step of the way. I wanted to be done with it already! I wanted to be anywhere and everywhere but where I was."

During her time of unemployment, Meg did a lot of personal work to learn how to slow down and bring her full presence to mundane tasks around the house as well as to more significant experiences. Recently, she remarked, "It's time to paint the spindles again. It's seven years later, and now I'm looking at those things, saying, 'No problem, when can I start?' I know I can show up now and not wish the whole time I were someplace else. Enough has changed internally that this time, it will be a pleasure."

In practicing presence, we are not so much addressing *what* we do as *how* we do it. This is about the quality of our energy as we move through our days—not just the special, extraordinary days but the ordinary ones. One of Vietnamese Zen master Thich Nhat Hanh's central teachings is about this mindful presence in everyday life:

> There are two ways to wash the dishes. The first is to wash the dishes in order to have clean dishes and the second is to wash the dishes in order to wash the dishes. . . . If while washing dishes, we think only of the cup of tea that awaits us, thus hurrying to get the dishes out of the way as if they were a nuisance, then we are not "washing the dishes to wash the dishes." What's more, we are not alive during the time we are washing the dishes. In fact we are completely incapable of realizing the miracle of life while standing at the sink. If we can't wash the dishes, the chances are we won't be able to drink our tea either.

While drinking the cup of tea, we will only be thinking of other things, barely aware of the cup in our hands. Thus we are sucked away into the future—and we are incapable of actually living one minute of life.[4]

The Tyranny of the List

It's humbling to realize how easy it is for our minds to be lost in stories about what happened yesterday or what we hope or fear for tomorrow while going through the motions of our days. It is as if we are on automatic pilot, not really seeing our children's faces, not really tasting our food as we eat, not really feeling the water on our hands as we wash the dishes, not really noticing much about life as we "live" it. Add to this a touch of speed from the pace of our culture, plus the omnipresent List of Things to Do, and we have what I call "list consciousness." List consciousness is a state of mind that is entirely future-oriented. With a subtle but constant quality of rushing, it operates on the premise that life will happen once everything is crossed off the List. (This, by the way, is itself an illusion. Even when we die, it is unlikely that everything will be crossed off the List!) When I am in list consciousness, it is as if I am out in front of myself or ahead of myself. I am leaning into the future and, in the process, completely missing the present.

Practicing presence is training in releasing ourselves from this mind-state. It punctures the fantasy that somehow life will begin when the kids' soccer season is over or when I lose ten pounds or when I get over this cold or even when I take that meditation course and learn how to be more present! Practicing presence is bringing ourselves to the recognition that life is happening right now—and it is inviting us to wake up and notice.

The Downside of Multitasking

Another mind-state that makes presence difficult is what we have come to call "multitasking." Multitasking is not technically doing several things simultaneously but rather switching attention rapidly between two or more things while keeping track of the status of all of them. It is not just a way of accomplishing tasks but also a mind-state because in order to do several things at once, we need to divide our attention, and this actually affects our brain. Studies show that in addition to reducing efficiency and effectiveness, multitasking can cause short-term memory problems and changes in the ability to con-centrate or gaps in attentiveness. Intense multitasking can also induce a stress response—that is, an adrenaline rush—that, when prolonged, can damage cells that form new memory. Based on his study of multitasking, Marcel Just of Carnegie Mellon University concludes, "It doesn't mean you can't do several things at the same time. But we're kidding ourselves if we think we can do so without cost."[5] Studies show the cost in terms of reduction in efficiency and difficulty in concentrating, among other things. Perhaps even more important, too much multitasking denies us the kind of experience that writer Henry Miller alludes to when he says, "The moment one gives close attention to anything, even a blade of grass, it be-comes a mysterious, awesome, indescribably magnificent world in itself."[6] To put it another way, multitasking can obliterate our ability to drop into the Deep River realm through the doorway of paying close attention to the present moment.

Practicing presence, then, is also training in releasing ourselves from multitasking. This practice encourages a way of doing things that is becoming increasingly rare in this information-saturated and speed-obsessed culture: doing one thing at a time, and taking our time to do it. The ability to do several things at once can be a very useful skill at times. The problem comes when we can't shift *out* of multitasking throughout the day, when it becomes a habit rather than a choice and we can't readily choose to focus attention on one sight, sound, sensation, person, task, or activity when we want or need to.

Here is a little exercise in practicing presence: next time you're hungry, instead of grabbing a "quick bite" while reading your mail while listening to the news while getting ready to be out the door to get the next errand done, try this: sit down while eating and taste your food while chewing it while noticing the sensations in your mouth while breathing. I call this simple practice "the new multitasking." You might be amazed to find that this is more than enough to do at once! (You will find more on eating with presence in the first exercise at the end of this chapter.)

Presence and the Deep River

The interconnectedness of practicing presence and touching the Deep River arises from three characteristics related to both:

- Moving from surface busyness to slowing down
- Moving from time-bound awareness to a sense of timelessness
- Moving from habitual seeing to seeing freshly, with "new eyes"

Presence and Slowing Down

Practicing presence doesn't necessarily take more time; it takes more *awareness* than we ordinarily bring to a given moment. However, when we are truly present, we tend to slow down. This is one reason that practicing presence acts as a doorway to the Deep River realm. As we saw in Chapter Two, slowing down is a key to unlocking Deep River access. Thus, almost anything that slows me down has the potential to help me drop into the Deep River dimension. In the context of the practice of presence, what I mean by "slowing down" is *not rushing*. You can be fully present and play a fast and intense game of ping-pong. (In fact, if you're *not* fully present, you're much more likely to miss a shot!) Presence and moving quickly can go together. But it's very difficult to be present while rushing. So the practice of presence curbs the tendency to rush when rushing isn't necessary. And when we are not rushing, it becomes easier for deeper currents to flow into our lives.

For Rebecca, a Deep River group member, racewalking is an activity that invites her into the here and now. Her experience of racewalking is a good example of moving quickly with presence, opening to the Deep River realm in the process. She explains:

When I'm racewalking, all my thoughts seem to quiet. I find that something opens up that allows me to be really present within my own body. I don't have extraneous thoughts, and time doesn't exist. It's just being. I can hear my heart beating, and I can feel my feet hitting the pavement. There's a rhythm that develops; my breathing starts to get in sync with the heart and the sound of my feet. My awareness opens up, but not in a cluttered way. It's like a channel opens and I feel a sense of freedom and a flow. . . . There's no real dividing line between where I leave off and the activity begins. It's almost like entering into an altered state. I hesitate to use that term because it implies it's something foreign or "away," whereas really it's coming into a more present state. But because it's not the norm, it feels "altered." In fact, it's more *me*.

The Timeless Present

When Rebecca practices presence through racewalking, she says that "time doesn't exist." In Chapter Two, I describe the altered sense of time that many women have during Deep River experiences. Time is described as slowing down, or opening up, or being suspended, or being infinite, and so on. This altered sense of time has to do with shifting out of time-bound list consciousness or multitasking and into the here and now. In making this shift, we drop into the timeless present, where a sense of flow, vitality, spaciousness—and other qualities of the Deep River—can arise naturally. Buddhist monk Amaro Bhikkhu says, "We sometimes think of the here and now as a minute, insignificant little line between a vast past and a vast future; however, the more we observe the mind the more we realize that the here and now is that which is vast and the past and future are like vague mirages. The now is vast and immeasurable, infinite. . . . In that timeless presence there is the quality of delight, the natural joy of the free mind."[7]

For many women in my groups, this sense of timelessness in the here and now is a key aspect of their contact with the Deep River. The activities they describe vary widely, from painting to gardening to writing to talking with a good friend to swimming, and so on. The common threads, regardless of what activity they engage in, are focused attention in the moment and freedom from the constraints of time. For Carrie, this happens when she sketches:

> When I draw in my sketchbook, time stands still. My attention is solely focused on the item I am drawing—its form, the way the light shimmers on the edge and then disappears into the shadows behind. I caress the paper with my pencil, following the curve of the bowl or the distant shore or treetop as best I can. It doesn't really matter what I am drawing; it is the act of drawing that calms my mind. Time stands still as I focus on shading, pattern, color. These drawings are not necessarily for others to see but are a way to drop into the Deep River and come out refreshed.

Seeing with New Eyes

Have you ever seen (or perhaps been) a parent rushing a young child along as he or she examines a leaf, rock, bug, shell, or other simple wonder of the world? This familiar scene is a good example of the difference between living in list consciousness and being in the here and now. When we are able to step into the present moment, not only does time release its hold on us, but we can see freshly, with a kind of childlike wonder, no matter what our age. With this kind of seeing, even ordinary things can look, as Henry Miller says, "indescribably magnificent." The ability to see in this way is important because it gives rise to appreciation and gratitude for small things, for what is right in front of us, for life just as it is. Without the ability to enter the present moment, a kind of restless desire often keeps us busy looking for the next thing that might stimulate our senses and satisfy the vague desire for something *more*, something other than what is right here, right now. We need to remind of ourselves of what French writer Marcel Proust said: "The real magic of discovery lies not in seeking new landscapes, but in having new eyes."[8]

Once, at the end of a group meditation session, I opened my eyes and directly in my line of vision was a pair of brown shoes that belonged to someone else in the group. They were truly nothing special, just a pair of somewhat worn brown shoes. My mind was quiet in that moment, and I simply looked at the shoes. They seemed beautiful to me; it wasn't that they were pretty or elegant or particularly well made. Their beauty had to do with what Buddhism would call their "suchness"—my sense of the shoes being exactly as they were, perfectly "themselves," if you will. This experience is hard to convey. I am describing a kind of seeing that is directly in the moment, without taking the moment or the sight for granted or overlaying it with the preoccupations and thoughts that often veil our vision. If anyone had asked me that night what the highlight of my day was, I definitely would have answered, "I saw a pair of brown shoes." This would have made no sense on its face, but it would have been true.

Beauty is in *how* we see, not *what* we see. The ability to live deeply and joyfully is based on *how* we experience things, not *what* things we experience. Jane Dobisz says, "Joy comes from appreciation. Appreciation comes from paying attention."[9] The practice of presence helps us give the kind of attention to ourselves, to others, and to our lives, just as they are, and that draws us toward joy.

Taming Self-Expectations and the Practice of Presence

Each of the practices in the last four chapters both supports and is supported by the practice of presence. Implicit in taming expectations is the fact that when our expectations are high and prominent, they can take us away from the present moment. Instead of appreciating where we are, we live in some imagined future made up of how we want ourselves or our life to be rather than how they actually are. I once saw a billboard outside a church that said, "To dream of the person you want to become is to waste the person that you are." If we can tame our expectations about our dreamed-of lives, we are more likely not to waste the preciousness of the present moment. Carol, who spoke of self-expectations in the preceding chapter, explains the connection for her:

I am becoming more aware of how running to keep up with my self-expectations, my image of what I should be doing at any moment in time, actually clouds my vision and keeps me from being fully (if at all) engaged in what is really going on. Self-expectations keep me from being present in the moment. If I am so focused on my work, I run the real risk of missing out on my own life. How often have I told my kids "Not now, I have work to do"? Too often. And I am doing the work in large part for their benefit. How odd, when in fact part of what I see as my life's work is caring for them, being present with them. I am working on easing up on my expectations and just showing up for as many moments as I can. Easier said than done, but a worthy goal!

Taming self-expectations makes it easier to be present, and conversely, being present reduces the preoccupation with expectations. This is because, in fact, we can't be fully in the present moment and hold an expectation for the future at the same time. If I am savoring the taste of a mouthful of out-of-this-world crème brûlée, by the time I have the thought "I should learn how to make this" or "This is going straight onto my hips," I am no longer in the present. But if, say, this is the first time I have ever tasted crème brûlée, and I happen to be tasting it at the first meal of my first trip to France, in a fabulous restaurant in Paris, the excitement and newness of the situation might bring me so fully into the present that thoughts about trying to make this at home or future results of how many calories I might be ingesting don't even come into my mind. The richness of the here and now crowds out future-oriented self-expectations.

Befriending Feelings and the Practice of Presence

Being present allows us to embrace life wholeheartedly. If we can't inhabit the present moment, we don't really inhabit our lives. It's easy to feel the desire to enter fully into life during good times. But what happens when our experience in the moment is grief or anger or fear, loneliness, boredom, shame? We tend to be fair-weather friends to the moment and attempt to exit the present promptly when we feel painful or difficult emotions. But it isn't possible to filter out what we don't find agreeable and still be present and truly open to life. Thus, learning to stay with uncomfortable feelings is important in helping us cultivate presence.

The converse is also true: when we are in the here and now, difficult feelings are easier to be with. This may not be obvious at first. But if you examine your experience carefully, you'll notice that often the desire to escape a difficult feeling comes not from the emotion itself but from the *thought* that the feeling will go on and on, or that it will hurt too much, or some other, often future-oriented thought about the feeling. (This is often true for physical as well as emotional pain.) As we saw in Chapter Six, thoughts *about* feelings are not the same as the direct experience of the feelings themselves (which necessarily takes place in the present moment). The nature of feelings, when we allow them to, is to move and change. Staying with our direct moment-to-moment experience of a feeling, we can notice how and when it changes and often there is no need to try to escape from it. Meditation teacher Michele McDonald says, "When we have difficult times in our life, the only refuge there is, is to connect to the present moment. We struggle like a fish out of water, and we finally learn that the refuge *is* being in the present moment, going *through* the experience, as best we can."[10]

Making Boundaries and the Practice of Presence

The ability to make boundaries also helps us enter the present moment. Saying "yes" when I mean "yes" makes it easier to show up for whatever I'm doing, because I have *chosen* to be where I am. On the other hand, if I say "yes" when I mean "no," I am likely to "check out," or not be fully present, because I'm not where I mean to be or want to be. Recently, a friend of mine wanted to stop in and say "hello" after returning from a trip. I wanted to see her, but it wasn't a good time for me. I said "yes," and then immediately felt divided. I knew from past experience that if she came, I would be only half present because I had said "yes" when I meant "no." So I called her back and arranged a time when I could be 100 percent present.

Chapter Five addresses making boundaries in our outer world—that is, saying "no" to people, things, and activities in order to be less fragmented and more in touch with what's important in our daily lives. But practicing presence involves *inner* boundary making as well, saying "no" to what poet Mary Oliver calls "the intimate interrupter." She writes about the need for solitude in creative work and how the phone or a visitor can interrupt the creative flow. Then she explains a different kind of interruption:

> But just as often . . . the interruption comes not from another, but from the self itself, or some other self within the self, that whistles and pounds upon the door panels and tosses itself, splashing, into the pond of meditation. And what does it have to say? That you must phone the dentist, that you are out of mustard, that your uncle Stanley's birthday is two weeks hence. You react, of course. Then you return to your work, only to find that the imps of the idea have fled back into the mist.
>
> It is this internal force—this intimate interrupter—whose tracks I would follow. The world sheds . . . its many greetings, as a world should. . . . But that the self can interrupt the self—and does—is a darker and more curious matter.[11]

This "darker and more curious matter" is simply what our minds do. To stay present, we need to have some ability to focus or concentrate our minds. Concentration is a kind of inner boundary making—saying "yes" to the object of our concentration and "no" to everything else that shows up. (Fortunately, concentration can be cultivated, and there are many time-tested methods for doing so; the Selected Reading lists some of the many resources on the subject.)[12]

Just as making inner and outer boundaries can help us come fully into the present, we strengthen our boundary-making ability every time we bring ourselves into the here and now. This is because we must say "no" to the past and the future in order to be in the present. Marsha, a Deep River group member, describes this process:

There are times when my son wants me to read to him and I *do* have time, but I also have a lot on my list. At first, I feel his request as getting in the way of my momentum to work. But I also know that spending time reading to him is more important than getting the next thing done. So I agree to read, but there's an edge of trying to get it over with, and I'm only half there. The rest of me is planning, thinking ahead, plotting out the rest of the evening. Then, sometimes, I can actively shift out of this divided place. I make a *choice* to set the list aside, and I focus on him. I look at him, see his face, and I am actually fully there, reading a book to my son. I think he can tell the difference, and I *know* I can tell the difference.

The "choice" Marsha describes is an act of boundary making, saying "no" to the future and "yes" to the now, which allows her to be present with her child.

Taking Time-In and the Practice of Presence

The first practice, taking time-in, also supports the ability to be present. It's not necessary to do a meditation or concentration practice that explicitly cultivates presence while taking time-in. We invite ourselves into the present moment simply by having a time each day when we are not multitasking and when we intentionally cut down on distraction. For example, Leslie knits during her time-in: "I choose beautiful yarns and simple patterns so that I can just knit effortlessly. The repetitiveness of the stitches, the feel of the yarn, the richness of the color all serve to quiet my mind." As Leslie puts it, being fully present with the sensations of knitting is her way of "dipping into the Deep River at night, once the kids are in bed and the lights turned off on all the work that didn't get finished."

Being present can also support the practice of time-in. If we are awake and paying attention to what is happening in ourselves and our lives, it is more likely that we will know when we are in need of alone time. We will know when we have stayed overlong on the surface and need to drop down to the Deep River realm. If we perpetually distract ourselves, we may not see or hear the signals that call us inward.

Practicing Presence

So how do we practice presence? The first step is to understand the value of paying attention. I hope it is clear by now that this practice doesn't just help with inadvertently bumping into doors or spilling coffee. Paying attention in the present moment invites a deeper, richer quality of life, the quality of life we seek in drawing from the Deep River. Henry David Thoreau said, "Only that day dawns to which we are awake."[13] This wisdom, gleaned from Thoreau's solitary retreat on Walden Pond, intimates that the practice of presence is not even just about a better *quality* of life; it is at the heart of being truly alive.

Once there is understanding about the value of practicing presence, the next step is to do just what it says: practice. Given that there is no better time to practice than *now*, take a moment, after you read these next words, to shift your attention from reading to noticing that you are breathing. Feel your body sitting, making contact with whatever you are sitting on, and notice the sensations of breathing. Allow these sensations—at your nostrils, in your chest, in your abdomen—to come into the foreground of your awareness. Notice any other body sensations you are aware of as you breathe. Now gently expand your awareness to a sense of your whole body, sitting, breathing, here, now.

Bringing attention to the present moment unclutters your mind. Awareness of breathing is a very immediate—and always available—way to experience this uncluttering effect. A very simple way to encourage presence is to intentionally pause at the beginning or the end or in the midst of an activity—and pay attention to your breath. Even just a few moments of mindful attention to your breathing can quiet a chattering mind and be surprisingly refreshing. Because most of us have a tendency to get lost in the workings of our mind, bringing attention to what we are receiving through one or more of our senses—hearing, seeing, smelling, tasting, touching—is an effective doorway into the here and now. In the exercise section, you will find more ways to practice presence.

Blocking Belief: "The grass is greener any place but here, any time but now."

It's easy to understand the desire to get lost in fantasy about the past or future in the midst of a difficult life situation or while experiencing physical or emotional pain. But have you ever had an experience like this: you are walking on a beautiful wooded trail or watching a sunset over water or relaxing with good friends at the end of a day's work, doing something at least mildly enjoyable or pleasant, and you begin to think about the last time you did something like this or about what you're going to do when you get home or about how your cat needs her toenails cut. . . . Your mind takes you away from a present moment that is perfectly agreeable, in favor of a past or future moment that presumably was or will be better or more important than *this* moment.

As I mentioned earlier, this tendency for the mind to roam here and there and away from the moment is simply what minds do. But there is also an assumption implicit in the pull toward the past or future and away from the present that some *other* time must be more important than this moment. This underlying belief that the grass is always greener on the other side of here and now effectively blocks presence.

When I speak about presence in my groups, I use a cartoon by Gahan Wilson that shows two monks sitting side by side. The older, presumably wiser one is saying to the younger monk, who has a look of dismay on his face, "Nothing happens next. This is it."[14] It seems that we all, Zen monks included, tend to ignore the present as we look toward the next best thing or try to relive the last good thing. The first step in working with the grass-is-greener syndrome is to bring nonjudgmental awareness to this tendency. We can notice and name the restless desire for something more, something other than what this moment offers. We can breathe with that feeling, as we can with any other difficult or uncomfortable feeling, and be-friend it as best we can. The tendency to skip over the here and now is a deeply held habit of mind. We begin to loosen its grip by notic-ing when we seek to move away from presence, even if we can't bring ourselves back into the moment.

I have noticed an amusing pattern in my own mind that reminds me of the young monk. I meditate during my time-in in the morn-ing. Meditation, for me, is a helpful way to practice presence. As I sit, my mind goes on its little trips of planning, remembering, worrying, and so on. When I become aware that I'm rehearsing a conversation I'll be having with a colleague later or replaying—again—the last phone call with my daughter, I bring myself gently back, as best as I can, to simple awareness of my breath, my body, here, now. Recently, I noticed the irony of one of my little recurring mind trips. While meditating, I imagine how calm and mindful I will be when I get up from the cushion. I see myself slowly walking into the kitchen, fully present, feeling the floor under my feet with each step, feeling my whole body moving through space, taking in the colors and shapes of the house with my eyes as I mindfully walk from one room to the other. It's a lovely fantasy, but I chuckled to myself when I realized that there I was, meditating with no other intention than to be pres-ent, and my mind was off in the future, imagining how present I was *going to be*! This is the grass-is-greener syndrome. Thinking *about* being present in the moment is still thinking, not presence.

The remedy for the belief that the grass is greener any time but here, any place but now, is not another, more helpful belief. Once we become aware that we are acting as if some other time or place is where our attention ought to be, the remedy is closer than *any* thought or belief: the remedy lies in our ability to bring our atten-tion back to the present moment, here and now.

ཚ Exercise: The Amazing Eating-a-Raisin Experience

This exercise was created by Jon Kabat-Zinn for his Mindfulness-Based Stress Reduction program at the University of Massachusetts Medical Center. I like it because it has to do with eating—a common daily activity that can be fraught with emotional complexity, especially for women in this culture. This exercise offers a way of learning to unclutter the process of nourishing our bodies through the practice of presence.

1. To do this exercise, you will need a raisin and five or ten minutes of uninterrupted time. Sit with your raisin in a quiet spot, holding it in the palm of your hand. Take the time to really look at it; notice its texture, color, size, how the light reflects on its surfaces. As you do this, imagine that you are seeing this object in your hand for the first time. Imagine that you are looking at it as a young child might, with no name for it, no preconceptions about it, just clear, direct seeing of the object.

2. Pick it up between two fingers, and turn it over as you observe. See it from all sides, all angles. Notice what it feels like between your fingers. Explore it with your eyes and hands, seeing, touching. At any time, if you begin thinking about how long this is taking or what you'll be doing next or any other thought, just note that you are thinking and gently return your attention to the object.

3. Now, bring the object close to your nose and smell it. Take your time, and breathe in the smell. When you're ready, slowly put it in your mouth and notice how it feels. At first, without biting into it, notice what it feels like on your tongue. Then, for the sake of concentration on the sense of taste, close your eyes, bite it, and then slowly begin to chew it. Notice the flavor and the sensations in your mouth as you chew. Take your time, and stay with the tastes and sensations while you continue to chew and then as you swallow.

4. When you finish, allow yourself some time to sit quietly with your eyes closed. As the tastes and sensations fade from your mouth, just focus gently on your breathing for a few moments.

5. Whenever you're ready, open your eyes, and if you wish, make some notes about your experience. Did you notice anything

about this particular food that you never noticed or paid attention to before? Did you notice anything about the process of eating that you never noticed or paid attention to before? Is there anything from this experience of mindful eating that you would like to practice at mealtimes? If so, what?

⬥ Exercise: Practicing Presence in Daily Life

This exercise is given in the spirit of taking small steps. Even when you understand the importance of practicing presence, it's not necessarily helpful to try to be fully aware of every moment. Instead, I suggest thinking in terms of "moments of mindfulness" and small victories. This exercise gives a form for practicing presence during an ordinary daily activity.

1. Find a place where you can be undisturbed for five or ten minutes. Think about the activities of a typical day, with the intention of choosing one activity that you would like to bring the quality of presence to. Choose something simple, something you do every day. It could be taking your first sip of tea or coffee in the morning; it could be brushing your teeth, walking up your stairs, opening your front door, or turning the keys in your car's ignition. You could choose to be present to your breathing when you stop at a traffic light or when you kiss your child good night. You may think of many possibilities, but for now just choose one, something simple and routine. There is no one right choice.

2. When you have chosen an activity, close your eyes and take a little time to see and feel yourself, in your mind's eye, doing this one thing with presence. Imagine doing this activity as if it's the first time you've ever done it. Imagine doing it with the "new eyes" of a child. Imagine doing it with gratitude for the simple fact that you are alive and therefore able to do

this activity. Notice what it is like to bring your full attention to what you are doing. How do you experience it in your body? Imagine breathing fully as you do this activity. Take your time to complete the activity in your mind's eye. When you're ready, open your eyes and, if you wish, take some notes.

3. The visualization in step 2 is an intentional rehearsal of what it is like to pay attention in your daily life. For the next week, practice presence with your chosen activity. When you get carried away in thoughts, simply come back to what you are doing. You may wish to record your experience in your journal, including any commentary by your inner critic and whether you notice any carryover to other parts of your day. After a week, you can continue practicing with the original activity, add another, or switch to a new activity. Writer and teacher Roger Walsh notes that with exercises such as this one, "it soon becomes apparent that any normal activity can be transformed into a sacred ritual and a moment of awakening."[15]

Exercise: One Thing at a Time

This exercise draws on your ability to make boundaries in order to be present.

Choose a designated length of time—a whole day, a morning or afternoon, or even just one hour—during which you renounce multitasking and commit to doing only one thing at a time. This will mean saying "no" to reading the paper while eating, listening to the radio while driving, cleaning up the kitchen while talking on the phone. Bring as much presence as possible to a given activity as you do it. The commitment not to do other things simultaneously during your designated time will make it easier to be present. If you wish, record your experience in your journal. What effect does it have on you, on the things you do, on the people around you, to do one thing at a time?[16]

⚘ Exercise: The Imaginary Camera

The idea for this exercise came from Becky Allen Mixter, a woman in one of my groups; actually, it came from her father. When we talked about the practice of presence in the group, she was reminded of something her father did when she was growing up. Whenever the family was together and there was a special moment, he used his imaginary camera. When they were looking at a breathtaking view after a hike up a mountain or all coming together for their first meal after she and her siblings had been away, her father would raise his hands in front of his face as if he were holding a camera, and "take a snapshot." His message to his family was "Pay attention. Notice this moment; it's precious."

Often when we have actual cameras, we are too busy recording the moment (for some future time) to actually be present. The imaginary camera, on the other hand, is a means of saying, "Be fully here, now, in this precious moment." A noteworthy side effect of practicing presence in this way is that we tend to remember longer and more vividly those moments when we are fully present. Becky says her memories of the times when her father called the family into presence are "crystal clear to this day." Since then, she has taken many "snapshots" of her own: "driving around the corner to my house with my new baby asleep in the back of the car; watching my father read to my kids; the exhilaration of sailing on Lake Michigan; the innocence of my daughter's face just after she'd fallen asleep in my arms."

When we are looking for them, precious moments abound. Keep your imaginary camera with you at all times. Whether you actually bring your hands in front of your face and click, or just imagine doing so, taking a "snapshot" of precious moments will help bring your focus to the here and now.

―――――――

When I realize I'm on automatic pilot or I find myself in list consciousness or my mind says the grass is greener "there, then" while my body is "here, now," I think of a haiku that was written by the Japanese poet Basho over three hundred years ago:

> *Even in Kyoto—*
> *Hearing the cuckoo's cry—*
> *I long for Kyoto.*[17]

It helps me to know that humans have been working with these habits of mind for centuries. It helps me soften toward myself and smile inwardly at my chattering mind. And sometimes, it helps me slow down and wake up to this very moment.

Chapter Nine

Do Something You Love

Whatever is deeply loved—friends, grandchild,
late afternoon light, masonry, tennis, whatever
absorbs you—this may be a reflection of how you
move in the invisible world of spirit. It is your
beauty, the elegant point where everything is one.
—*Coleman Barks*, The Illuminated Rumi

One evening about a year after our first child was born, my husband and I had some precious time by ourselves. We went out to dinner, where the conversation turned to reviewing the year and sharing hopes and plans for the coming months. I don't remember much of what we talked about, but I do remember this: seemingly out of the blue, he said to me, "I'm pretty sure I married a person who knew how to have fun. Where did she go?" I was surprised by his words, but as I considered them, I realized this comment wasn't coming out of the blue. The responsibilities of new motherhood had so consumed my time, energy, and attention that I wasn't even aware that the fun side of me had virtually disappeared.

Since then, I have listened to countless women tell some version of this same story in relation to child rearing or work or both. It seems that in the face of the needs of others and the responsibilities in our lives, we quite easily lose sight of having fun, of what truly nurtures us, of what we love to do. Of course, maturity involves assuming responsibility—being accountable for one's own actions, being dependable in relation to others—and also being response-able—that is, able to respond to others. All of these traits are not only desirable but essential for those who care for babies and children. As women, we are socialized early to attend to others' needs. For our children's sake and for the health and well-being of our species, this is a good thing. It can also be deeply meaningful and gratifying for us personally. But over the years, I have seen many, many women fall into a pattern of being so focused on the needs of their children or their partners or their bosses, coworkers, friends, relatives—even their pets—that they lose the capacity to play, to do things just for fun.

The Renewing Power of Joy

Doing something you love is one of the six practices for touching the Deep River within because when we do something simply for enjoyment, it replenishes us, it refills our well. We are rejuvenated, in part, because when engaged in an activity we really love, we are drawn into the present moment *effortlessly*. Whether playing tennis, conversing with a dear friend, learning how to quilt, or listening to a symphony, doing a loved activity focuses attention in the here and now, where time releases its hold. Without having to try hard or go anywhere, we get a vacation from both list consciousness and multitasking.

Also, with this practice, we allow ourselves leisure in the sense that the Greeks meant it—the kind of freedom from the demands of work and obligation that revitalizes, brings forth creativity, encourages learning, and allows imagination and inspiration to flourish. This might mean playing the piano (especially when not a Musician), drawing or painting (especially when not an Artist), bird-watching or dancing or arranging flowers just for the fun of it. When time is short and the list is long, it's typical to eliminate these kinds of activities— things that we *enjoy* doing but that are not necessarily *purposeful*. As writer and peace activist Jim Rice puts it, "Leisure involves the freedom to engage in any art or skill that's not a means to an end—in other words, an activity that is pursued for the sheer joy of it."[1]

Astrid began to dance at a time in her life when there was close to no joy. She'd stopped working in order to be at home with her two young children, but she found full-time parenting a challenge, and her marriage was strained. Her days were filled with caretaking: "I was constantly on duty for the kids, trying to make my husband happy, keeping lists, maintaining the house, the car, the bills. I was also involved in church outreach and community service. My life was a series of responsibilities, all piling up." Astrid says she was look-ing for change and began to ask herself, "What makes me happy?" She identified dance, which she had loved as a child but stopped when she was twelve, in response to her mother's criticism.

It took Astrid a couple of years to actually enroll in a dance class. She tried a few different classes before she found her true love: the Argentine tango. "There are steps to learn, but it's also a lot about feeling the music and improvising." The challenge of learning the steps in combination with lots of freedom to improvise struck just the right balance for her. She describes the beginning of her love af-fair with tango: "At first, I went incognito. This was something just for me, and I wanted to keep it separate from the rest of my life. I didn't tell anyone there where I was from, and none of my friends or family knew I was doing it. No one was judging me. So if I couldn't learn these dance steps, who cared?"

By this time, she and her husband had separated, and Astrid was struggling financially. She could barely afford the fee for lessons, but dancing the tango was essential for her. She says, "For one hour a week, I gave myself to something I loved. When everything else was draining me, this made me happy. It was exciting to learn the steps, and I always felt recharged afterward. It was like having a tiny little night-light on in the dark. . . . That one hour a week pulled me out of a gray, dark fog."

For Astrid, dancing was a lifeline when she was struggling through a very difficult time. It's not necessary, of course, to wait for bleak times to hit before you start doing something you love; this practice can bring benefits during the garden-variety ups and downs of normal life, too. As we saw in Chapter Seven, the practice of taming self-expectations can help you lighten up internally, softening and warming what can be quite a harsh and unforgiving inner climate when the critic is in control. Doing something you love has a similar lightening effect, except from the outside in. When we take time to dance, take photographs of people on a city street, collect rocks on a beach, or "play dress-up" at a thrift store, the List seems less overwhelming afterward. Doing something you love can bring the qualities of play, creativity, fun, silliness, excitement, inspiration, passion, beauty, and enjoyment into your life. It's a cure for taking life too seriously. Without having something you love to do somewhere in your schedule, the activities that fill your days—including the Deep River practices—run the risk of adding up to life as one long, burdensome list of things to do. Many women say they are seeking more balance in their lives; rarely do they mean, "I need to balance out too much enjoyment of life with more duty and responsibility."

Workaholism and Other Obsessions

One of Dee's true loves is reading. She loved to read as a child, but now she says she doesn't take time to read, except right before bed. Dee recently took a vacation in honor of her fiftieth birthday. She described it as "glorious, just *exactly* what I wanted to do." She lay on the beach for a week and just read. No books for work or for self-improvement, just novels and books that piqued her curiosity. When she got back home and wanted to incorporate reading time into her daily routine, she found it remarkably difficult to do. She said, with considerable frustration, "Can't I do something I love? Why do I think of it as 'stealing' time? I'm doing all this other stuff—for what? It doesn't make sense. If I can't get some enjoyment out of thirty minutes in my day, some real enjoyment, then what is the point of working like this? Am I going to wait for the next vacation, in a *year*?"

Dee is not alone in her dilemma. Some women are better than others at making time for the things they love to do. But we all suffer to some extent from a preoccupation with work—both the kind we get paid for and the work we do in our constant quest to improve ourselves. The fact that doing something you love must be named as a practice is a symptom of our work-obsessed culture. In a more natural rhythm, periods of work would alternate with periods of play and rest; we would accomplish a task, then celebrate, make music, dance, make love. While we haven't lost this rhythm altogether, our society values work most highly; play—or even nontask or non-achievement-oriented activity—is an afterthought. According to the organization Take Back Your Time, not only are we working more hours now than we did in the 1950s, but we are working more than the citizens of any other industrial country, and even more than medieval peasants did! Since women in the United States have joined the workforce in substantial numbers, many of us are doing double duty, working at work and working at home, making it even harder to allow ourselves time for personal enjoyment. While some women are fortunate enough to enjoy their job, doing a loved activity that is entirely free of the pressure of responsibility offers a kind of replenishment that is difficult to get on the job.

One symptom of our culturewide work obsession is that many of us don't take time off even when it's ours to take. In a *Boston Globe* article on overworked Americans, one software company employee said she rarely took her three weeks of paid vacation because of the grinding work ethic in her office, where almost no one used all of his or her allotted vacation time.[2] A 2004 study by the Families and Work Institute bears this out, finding that more than one-third of employees did not plan to use the full number of days of their *paid* vacation time.[3] Women in the study proved to be more overworked than men, yet women were shown to spend less time than men relaxing and enjoying themselves on vacation and more time meeting family responsibilities. (The study doesn't include full-time mothers, for whom "vacation," unless it is without the kids, is generally full-time work, albeit in a different setting.) I mention these statistics as a reminder of the power of the our culture to affect not only the way we work but also our relationship to leisure time.

"Whatever Is Deeply Loved"

Doing something you love is a Deep River practice, first, because it can provide balance and lighten the sense of burden that often accompanies a duty-filled schedule and a duty-filled frame of mind. Second, doing something you love is a Deep River practice because what we love often arises out of who we are, or as Coleman Barks puts it, what we love "may be a reflection of how [we] move in the invisible world of spirit." In this sense, doing something you love is a potential doorway to the Deep River realm. There is a connection between doing a loved activity and our very being. To say it another way, the things we love are tangible expressions of our intangible essence.

As I was thinking about how to explain this, what came to mind were obituaries. Besides naming the person's relatives and their achievements, the most common item used to describe and honor a person in their obituary is what they loved to do. It may be impossible to truly describe, much less to fully know, who any of us is in our essence as a unique being with a unique human life. But remembering that this person loved gardening or that person loved bull terriers, she loved Gothic architecture or he loved watercolor painting is part of saying, "This is who this person was."

Making time to do something you love is a way of honoring and expressing who you are while you are still alive. When we give ourselves permission to do a loved activity, the outer and inner aspects of who we are become aligned. Women in my groups describe the result of this alignment in different ways: as a sense of wholeness or "rightness," as deeply satisfying, nourishing, energizing, or enlivening. As I see it, these words describe the flow of the Deep River into their lives through doing something they love.

This alignment of inner and outer happened for Madeleine during the course of a Deep River group. Madeleine was married, had one child, and worked in a small software company. She came to the group because her job consumed much of her time and energy and she felt drained and out of touch with what she called "the river of light"—her words for the spiritual dimension of life, which had always been important to her. The group gave Madeleine the support structure she needed to reconnect with herself and her river of light. Madeleine began simply by carving out time for time-in once a week. Her husband agreed to take their daughter out on Saturday morning so that she could be at home by herself.

The first Saturday morning that Madeleine had time alone and quieted her thoughts, she realized that the time had come to watch a videotape that had been given to her two years earlier. Her best friend had made the tape before she died of breast cancer, telling Madeleine not to look at it until she was ready. She watched the tape twice, taking in her friend's loving messages and heartfelt advice, and cried pretty much all morning. Madeleine's words brought tears to the eyes of group members as she recounted the story of her morning.

The next week, Madeleine looked unusually animated. She reported that she had had her Saturday morning alone again, and this time, she had begun to act on something her friend had said to her on the tape. Her friend's message was "Keep writing the book." The other group members looked at her quizzically, and Madeleine explained that nine years ago, she had started to write a novel. "Then," she said, "I got married, and then I had a child, and then I started this job, and the book kind of got shelved in the midst of my new life."

It turned out that the book had literally been shelved; she had put the beginnings of it in a box on the top shelf in her closet. During that Saturday time-in, she had taken it down for the first time in nine years. "I read what I've written so far, and I really liked it," she said. "Then I picked up where I left off and started working on it."

Madeleine's face was glowing as she talked about the writing. It was clear to everyone in the room that this was a deep passion for her, and being reunited with it was like meeting a lover after a long time apart. She said, "All this week, I actually set my alarm for 4 A.M. so that I could write before I had to get ready for work. I know I can't keep this up, but I actually haven't been tired at all."

Madeleine was experiencing the powerful surge of energy that can be accessed when we do something we truly love. After this initial reconnection with her passion, she began to look at how to restructure her life to allow writing back into it on a regular basis.

What Gets in the Way?

There are times in life when a passion must go on the back burner. It's unlikely that with a newborn, for instance, Madeleine could have or even would have wanted to pursue her writing wholeheartedly. Lack of time and energy in certain life stages or circumstances sometimes precludes doing what we love while we fulfill responsibilities. But other obstacles can be overcome, once we become aware of them. Three important obstacles we can overcome are

- Confusing excellence with passion
- Not knowing what you love to do
- The inner critic (again)

Confusing Excellence with Passion

This may be obvious, but it bears mentioning: what we do well is not necessarily where our passion is. This is important for two reasons. The first is that when a person is good or gifted at something, she, and the people around her, may assume that that activity is what she loves. It's wonderful when being good at something and loving to do it go together, but when they don't, a lot of time and energy may go into developing a talent that gives little satisfaction because it is not what makes the heart sing. Astrid, for example, is an extremely organized person. For her, throwing together an event, even for large numbers of people, is second nature. Because it was easy for her, a lot of her volunteer community work involved organizing events. While being able to use her organizational skills for a good purpose was satisfying, it was not her true passion, and it didn't leave her feeling revitalized. When she found dance, Astrid learned to set limits on community work so that she had time to tango.

The second, perhaps more important reason not to confuse excellence with passion is that you may turn away from something that doesn't come naturally or that you're not highly gifted at but that will give you deep inner satisfaction. Loving to paint, for example, doesn't mean you have to be recognized by others as an Artist. While it is always gratifying to be recognized, the real joy comes in the *process* of painting, not necessarily in the product.

In her book *Nature and Other Mothers,* writer Brenda Peterson includes a beautiful essay about her high school passion of playing the clarinet. She was in the lowly third clarinet section of the orchestra, but she describes playing her part "with the happy abandon that always made my music teacher grimace slightly, her way of reminding me that excitement is not technique."[4] She describes having a realization while listening to a solo by the orchestra's revered first clarinetist; although she deeply appreciated the music and his playing, she would never be able to play the way he could. In self-conscious, rebellious misery, she began to skip practice and cancel lessons and came very close to selling her clarinet.

As she prepared to pass her beloved instrument over to a friend, she burst out crying. Through her tears came the understanding that "I had to play whatever instrument was mine, body and soul. I had to play because music was a way I would take in and give back to the world; it was the same as breathing."[5] She continues, "Since [then], I've often reckoned with the fact that . . . whatever passion I choose may not choose me. But if it's a choice between returning to that greater symphony or being forever lonely for a part of myself cast off simply because it is not a great gift, then let me keep my little chair . . . and there let me always hear the holy music; let me play my imperfect part."[6]

This is wisdom, to recognize that when we cut ourselves off from something we love because we're not brilliant at it, we are actually casting off a part of ourselves. Not only do we lose a source for experiencing joy, but we diminish our own sense of wholeness in rejecting that vital and imperfect part.

Not Knowing What You Love

It may sound strange, but many women don't readily know what they love to do. What you truly love is not necessarily what you "should" love or what is politically correct to love or what your spouse or child or best friend loves to do. Some of us have taken our cues from others for so long that we don't have much experience in listening to our own inner promptings about what we love.

In addition, the process of socialization often involves suppressing or rechanneling what we love. For example, if a three year-old's passion is to make mud pies, mom or dad might find that activity too messy and put a rapid stop to it. As we get older, other passions may be squelched in favor of "practicality" ("You can't make a *living* as an artist!") or because they conflict with family norms ("We just don't *do* bowling. What's wrong with tennis?"). Eventually, we may incorporate these kinds of messages into our own thinking, so that they become our own taboos. Then, we have little awareness of certain passions because we have learned to deny or reject them. If, while we are growing up, what we want or what we love to do is met at every turn with negativity or rejection, it may be particularly difficult as adults to ask, "What do I love to do?" and allow a true passion to surface. For example, Jody was a client who came to me because, despite a successful career and a good marriage, she felt depressed a lot of the time. Jody was the oldest of four children raised by a single mother who worked two jobs during most of Jody's childhood. She learned at a young age how to be responsible and to put her wants and needs aside. This was simply a survival strategy for Jody, as it is for many children who grow up in homes dominated by overwhelmed parents, by overbearing parents, or by highly needy parents. When these children's needs and wants are ignored or discounted again and again, over time, it becomes easier for the children to "not want" or not be aware of what is wanted, because that is less painful than wanting things they won't get. An important part of Jody's healing was learning to listen for, allow, and respond to her own desires and wants. She started with very basic questions like "What do I *want* to eat for dinner tonight?" Gradually, as she allowed herself to *have* wants and began to find ways to respond to them, either on her own or with others, her depression began to lift.

If you are not sure about what you love to do, beginning to simply consider the question "What makes me happy?" is a way to start breaking through the barriers to knowing. Asking yourself gently, without judgment, is helpful. This question is worthy of reflection, and sometimes it's necessary to look back in time, perhaps as far back as childhood, to uncover or rediscover authentic loves. The exercises at the end of this chapter will help you further explore finding and doing something you love.

That Same Old Voice Again!

It should come as no surprise that the inner critic has its ways of infiltrating the activities we do for fun and enjoyment. The critic plays a part when we give up a passion with the idea that we're not good enough at it or because those around us might not approve of it. It's a bit easier to quiet the critic's withering voice when we engage in an activity we love simply for the joy of it, without achievement-oriented goals. This is not to say that working toward mastery can't be fun; it can. But when we attach expectations of attainment to a passion, we need to be alert to the joy-deadening effect of the inner critic's judgments.

Kelsey's story is a cautionary tale about passion and the inner critic. Kelsey loved to sing as a child. She had the good fortune of being naturally talented at what she loved best, for she had a beautiful, powerful singing voice. She sang in choruses and musicals all through high school and college, then went on to a master's program in which she began to train for opera.

In graduate school, Kelsey's dream of singing professionally began to lose momentum. The world of opera is intensely competitive, and Kelsey's sensitivity to criticism was activated over and over. As she was growing up, her home environment—high expectations that as the oldest of six, she would take on responsibilities, yet very little encouragement or attention from either parent—had nurtured her inner critic. Kelsey was extremely hard on herself, so when she was critiqued by a voice teacher, she was doubly devastated—first by the teacher and then by her internal self-criticism.

Finally, after a particularly difficult lesson with a demanding teacher that left Kelsey in tears, she quit the program. This was the beginning of a dark period in her life. Her dream of singing opera had died, but more significant for her sense of well-being, she stopped singing altogether. When she came for therapy, Kelsey had not sung at all for seven years—not in the shower or while alone in her car and certainly not in the presence of anyone else. Rather than generating joy, singing just brought up the pain of criticism and rejection, so Kelsey avoided it. At that point, other things in her life, professionally and personally, were not going well, either. It was as if when she had closed herself off from singing, her life force had been, to some degree, choked off too. The road back to health and wholeness included a lot of work with taming self-expectations. For Kelsey, the measure of her self-acceptance was tied to her willingness to sing again. To reclaim her voice—on many levels—Kelsey had to heal from and make peace with the hurts of both her childhood and her experience as a graduate student. Part of that process involved reconnecting with singing the way she had sung as a young child: unselfconsciously and for the sheer joy of it.

Over time, Kelsey did begin to sing again, first when alone and sure that no one could hear her, then, gradually, for others. She is in the process of shifting from the office work she has done for years, which gives her nothing except a paycheck, to teaching music and singing. In my view, her students are fortunate to have a teacher who understands so deeply what to do and what *not* to do in order to nurture the seed of a passion and help it to grow.

Blocking Belief: "Once everything is checked off the list, *then* I can have some fun."

I got together recently with a group of colleagues who knew I was writing a book but didn't know what the content was. When I explained it, one of them said, "Let's see if we can guess what the six practices are." This is a group of seasoned therapists who collectively have spent many decades in psychological and spiritual study and practice. In very short order, they had come up with five out of the six. The one they couldn't guess was doing something you love.

I found this so interesting. It made sense to them as soon as I said it, but even with prompting and hints, they didn't come up with it. Perhaps it is a regional issue, a reflection of New England's Puritan work ethic. Perhaps it is an indication that therapists are unusually poor at enjoying themselves! More likely, I think, doing something you love was not thought of because in this all-work, all-the-time culture, even those of us who consciously try to create balance in our lives may not readily see our passions or the need to play as priorities.

In an environment in which time is chronically short and high value is placed on purposeful activity, the blocking belief "Once everything is checked off the list, *then* I can have some fun" is often present. "Once I clean the house and do the laundry, *maybe* there will be time for a quick visit to the garden." "If I have time after I take the kids to their music lessons, I might be able to sit down at the piano myself before starting dinner." Implicit in this way of allocating—or not allocating—time to do something you love is the belief that it's just not as important as the things that need to get done. "If I take time to go to the museum, one of my very favorite things to do, then I won't get the papers graded (the car washed, the bills paid)"—that is, "I won't get the more 'important' things done."

This blocking belief, like many others, derives its power from the fact that it contains a grain of truth. It is likely true that if you are reading this, you have more responsibilities and things on your list than you have time for. So it would appear that there really is no time to commit to simple, nonpurposeful enjoyment. One step toward releasing this blocking belief is to recognize that doing something you love belongs in the category of important but not urgent activities (see Chapter Five). Playing cards or attending a concert or mountain climbing is never urgent the way paying bills is urgent; therefore, task-oriented priorities can easily take precedence. But it *is* important; it's important because it nourishes the spirit and enables us to enjoy the life we have been given. In addition, doing something you love has an important side effect. It is *energizing*. When Madeleine began to write again, it was as if her battery had been recharged. She needed less sleep, and she gained energy for her job and other responsibilities as well as for writing. Astrid says that when she comes home from dancing, she is "all fired up" and has so much energy that she doesn't go to sleep for several hours, even if she was tired before she went to class. In this way, sometimes taking time to do something we love actually ends up giving us time because it gives us energy. When Deep River nourishment comes to us because we have aligned the inner and outer part of ourselves by doing something we love, we gain vitality. It's easy to forget this when we get locked into the List.

For those who hold dearly to the belief that work should always come before play, let me be clear: I am not espousing hedonism or advocating shirking responsibilities. I am also not recommending procrastination through doing things that are neither important nor urgent (watching TV on April 14 rather than doing taxes, for example). I *am* suggesting that we question the assumption that in order to be efficient and effective in our lives, to do things the right way or the best way, we need to postpone joy.

If you recognize in yourself the tendency to let things you enjoy fall off your list, I invite you to experiment with substituting a new belief for "Once everything is checked off the list, *then* I can have some fun." Try something along these lines: "Doing something I love gives me energy to live my life." Or one that was given to me on a rubber stamp: "Don't postpone joy." Or a paraphrase of Alan Watts: "Life is like music; you don't just play it to get to the end."

You can use one of these phrases or find one of your own that reminds you of the value of making room for something you love.

⚘ Exercise: What Do I Love?

This exercise draws from a method that Julia Cameron uses to help unlock creativity in her book *The Artist's Way*.[7] Her exercises, and this one, are designed to help bypass the voice of the Censor or the inner critic by asking yourself a question and rapidly answering it several times, without time to overthink the answers. In this case, the purpose is to help uncover, discover, or remember what you love to do.

1. Begin with four sheets of paper or four pages in your journal. Leave space at the top of each page, and insert numbers from 1 to 5 below the space. Go back to the first page, and in the space at the top, write this question: "What would I love to do if I had all the time, money, and energy I needed?" Don't be ponderous; just write whatever comes to mind. Take about a minute to write five answers—for example,

   1. Climb the Himalayas
   2. Paint watercolors on the Italian Riviera
   3. Open an antique store
   4. Start my own clothing line
   5. Collect antique musical instruments

2. Go on to the next page, and write the next question: "What would I love to do if I didn't care what other people thought?" Jot down answers 1 to 5, as quickly as possible. Don't worry if you write an answer more than once. Just put down whatever comes to mind—for example,

   1. Dye my hair red
   2. Paint my living room teal
   3. Take singing lessons
   4. Try gambling
   5. Wear lacy dresses

3. Now go on to the third page, and write the third question: "What would I love to do if it weren't too selfish?" Jot down five answers that come to mind—for example,

1. Hire a babysitter so I can go to bed (go to the library, go to a coffee shop) and read a novel
2. Take singing lessons
3. Make a space in my home just for me (my projects, my time-in)
4. Get season tickets to the symphony
5. Plan a vacation in Italy—and go!

4. Last but not least: "What did I used to love doing that I don't have time for now?" ("Used to" can mean any time in your past, from recently to as far back as childhood.) Write your answers as quickly as possible. Example:

1. Collect autumn leaves, press them, make leaf collages
2. Go country-western dancing on Friday nights
3. Have a pajama party
4. Spend a whole day at the beach
5. Bicycle to somewhere I've never been

5. Once you have completed all four pages, look back at your answers. What do you notice? Are there any patterns or themes? For example, are there groups of answers related to travel, music, or antiques, beautifying indoor space, physical challenges, or outdoor pursuits? Do your answers give you any new information about what you love to do? Is there any one of your answers that you could act on in the next week? For example, if "antiques" was a theme, could you carve out time to go antiquing in the next week, even if it's just window-shopping? If you loved spending the whole day at the beach as a child, you might plan to spend longer than you usually would next time you go to the beach, even if it can't be a whole day. If building sand castles was part of what made it special, bring a pail and shovel.

This exercise or any part of it can be repeated whenever you are feeling stuck, too laden with responsibilities, or out of touch with what you love to do.

─────────

❧ Exercise: The "What I Love" Collage

This exercise is another way to help you identify your passions and celebrate them. It is fun to do in a group, but you can also do it on your own or with your children. You will need a sheet of newspaper or a poster-sized piece of paper or cardboard, a glue stick or tape and scissors, and some old magazines.

1. Look through the magazines while holding in mind the question "What do I love?" or "What do I love to do?" Rip or cut out whatever images are intriguing, attractive, or interesting to you. Look for pictures of things that you know you love, but also be open to unexpected images. If you love to garden, for example, you might look for images of flowers or beautiful yards or grounds. But also choose images that you are drawn to without knowing why. This way, you might uncover something you love that you haven't been so aware of up to now. As in the preceding exercise, don't be ponderous. This exercise is meant to be done in the spirit of creative play.

2. Once you have a number of images, create a "what I love" collage by arranging and pasting or taping what you have cut out onto the large paper or cardboard. Put your collage where it can serve as a reminder of what you love to do.

Women in my groups love doing this exercise. For many, cutting and pasting and making a collage is the closest thing to play that they have experienced in months or years. Making the collage is a reminder in itself of how recharging it can be to do something for the fun of it.

─────────

༃ Exercise: Do It!

The preceding two exercises are designed primarily to help identify what brings you joy. The next step is to actually *do* what you love. This means, if you're not already doing so, creating time for whatever it is and making that time a priority—once a day, once a week, once a month, or whatever works for you. Once Astrid had identified dance as something she wanted to bring into her life, she says she figured it out "quantitatively." That is, she added up how much time all her responsibilities took in an average week ("including sleep!") and saw that she could take up to two hours, including travel time, for dance. My thinking process is not as quantitative as Astrid's, and yours may not be, either. But there are many other ways to find the time for something you love. The intention to do so is the most important factor in making it happen. If you need to, refer back to Chapter Five and use its principles of boundary making to help create time for something you love. Share your intention and plan with a friend or a Deep River buddy in order to gain support. Use your journal to name your intention, make your plan, and record your victories.

In closing this chapter, I want to emphasize again that the practice of doing something you love is about play, enjoyment, and lightness. If we remember to think of it that way, finding and doing what gives us joy might be easier and closer than we think. By way of illustration, here is a short account of how one Deep River group participant rediscovered a simple source of joy that had been buried for years:

> It was a midwinter day, just after a big New England snowstorm, when I worked my way through getting my children in snowsuits and then, mercifully, for once, dropped my to-do list and went tobogganing, with no deadlines in mind. At the top of the hill, underneath a bright, blue sky, I was grateful for the day, grateful for the opportunity to be out with my kids. As I sledded down the hill with my six-year-old son in front of me, I was shrieking with glee over the jumps and

bumps with a huge smile on my face. Evidently, I hadn't smiled like that in a while, because at the end, my son looked up, squeezed my hand, and said, "Is this what you loved to do when you were little?" I was so touched to see him so happy at seeing me so happy that I resolved to make room for that place of spontaneous joy more often!

Part Three

Keeping the
Deep River Flowing

The practices offered in the six chapters of Part Two provide effective tools for recovering balance, depth, and meaning in our individual lives. As we engage in bringing more sanity to our own daily living, questions often arise about another kind of balance: the balance between self and other, between our individual lives and the collective life of the groups, communities, and world we are part of. So much of what I have laid out in these pages encourages turning inward, while so much in our world needs attention and healing. Is Deep River work just glorified navel-gazing, letting the rest of the world go to hell? Is it more selfishness, which we need a lot *less* of if we wish to collectively find peace and healing? I think these are fair questions. If we care about the world we live in and the world we will leave to future generations, it is important to understand how the benefits of the Deep River practices extend beyond ourselves.

The purpose of Part Three, the final chapter, is to address how our inner work ripples outward and to describe the part we can play in keeping the Deep River flowing through the lives of the next generation and beyond.

Chapter Ten

Beyond Self-Care

I have discovered that all human evil
comes from this
. . . being unable to sit still in a room.
—*Blaise Pascal*, Pensées

Where people have lived in inwardness
The air is charged with blessing and does bless;
Windows look out on mountains and the walls are kind.
—*May Sarton*, "The Work of Happiness"

A while ago, during a casual conversation at a party, a very pleasant man asked me what I do. I talked about my private psychotherapy practice and then briefly described my Deep River groups. "Oh," he said, "I see; so you're helping women do nice things for themselves, like take bubble baths."

I'm not sure whether the problem was with what I said or how I said it or what he heard or all of the above, but it was clear to me that he did *not* understand what I was talking about. While the work of touching the Deep River is in part about self-care, its implications reach far beyond any individual woman's ability to relax and nurture herself. Yet in fairness to my fellow partygoer, I think it is quite easy to trivialize and misunderstand this work.

The potential impact of Deep River work on our communities, organizations, and society at large could be the subject of another whole book. Here, I simply want to touch on some of the ways that the benefits ripple outward much further than we might expect when we slow our pace and contact our inner selves. As part of considering how this work can help repair our world, we'll briefly explore its effect on our personal relationships and on our children and, therefore, on our future. In addition, we'll look at what's at stake if we don't find ways, collectively, to slow down. It's also important to consider the unique role that each of us can play in this healing, the role we are called to play as women, and how we can support one another as forces for good in the world. First, let's look closest to home, at the effect our own well-being has on our personal relationships.

Ourselves, Each Other

The ability to slow down and pay attention in the present moment, essential in Deep River practice, directly benefits our relationships. To put it simply, when we're going too fast, we risk running over each other. When we operate on automatic pilot, it's easy to hurt each other. When we're preoccupied with the ongoing chatter of the to-do list, we often don't hear each other. We slow down and practice presence not only to find ourselves but to find one another.

The great Catholic contemplative Thomas Merton said, "It is in deep solitude that I find the gentleness with which I can truly love my brothers."[1] This seeming paradox of deep connection to others while taking time-in has come up again and again in my personal and professional experience. Not only does this sense of connection to others *feel* good, but it also allows us to recognize our fundamental oneness as human beings. This recognition is the source of compassion and loving kindness that enables us to bridge the divides that separate us.

When I am having difficulty in a relationship, I typically fret or fume as I go through my day, doing other things and interacting with other people. Sometimes I will talk to my husband or a friend who can listen as I "talk out" what I'm feeling. Eventually, in most cases, I talk directly to the person about whatever is bothering me.

In my experience, the best outcomes from these conversations occur when I have stepped out of doing mode and taken some contemplative time-in before I talk to the person. Sometimes I write in my journal or meditate about the issue, or both. When I take the time to be alone with the difficulty, I often experience a change of heart, a softening, a new perspective. It may help me with problem solving, but the shift I experience goes beyond problem solving. When I tap into the waters of the Deep River, I have access to the gentleness that Merton speaks of, both toward myself and toward the other person. We may still disagree, but I no longer feel adversarial. I remember our common ground, and I can approach the other person with more openness and equanimity. The time I've spent on my inner work helps me become less polarized, so I can speak in a way that is easier to hear.

The interesting thing about all of this is that a change of heart toward another begins with a change of heart toward self. Seeing oneself clearly and with compassion is often the first necessary step in clearing the way for compassion toward others. We can find this clarity and compassion for ourselves when we slow down and make contact with the Deep River.

One Deep River group member says that when she incorporated time-in in her daily routine, it became easier to pause in the heat of the moment with her husband. "I can't say exactly why it works," she explains, "but I keep seeing it again and again, that there's a link between taking time to check in with myself and having some presence and compassion in the moment, instead of following a trajectory of my habitual response to be defensive and push people away." She describes an incident when she and her husband had had a tough day punctuated by a "blow-out fight" that was unresolved when she left for her weekly meditation group. "The group was really a chance to be with myself, to get quiet and take time-in. When I went home, I saw my husband looking devastated, like he'd been beaten up. I had the most compassionate reaction immediately. I went *toward* him instead of my usual pushing away. I sat down and told him how I *wished* the day had gone, instead of how it had. There is no way I would have had that response if I hadn't had the time-in. And by me reaching out, he totally came around, and he was grateful."

That taking time-in benefits our relationships is not a new idea, but it needs to be repeated and revisited because we so easily forget that our attitude toward ourselves affects our treatment of others. Slowing down and taking time to consider our feelings and actions can lead us to wiser, more considerate interaction. In our speeded-up culture, we have lost sight of the need to pause, to reflect, to incubate, not only for our own well-being but in order to give birth to harmony in our relationships and to wise action in the world.

Our Children, Our Future

When mothers in my groups stay on the topic of their children for too long, I usually steer them back to themselves, reminding them that this is an opportunity to step away from their children's needs and reconnect with their own inner lives, with what gives nourishment below the surface of their daily responsibilities. This prompting follows the model of the airlines' admonition to "secure your own oxygen mask first, then assist those next to you." Having said that, it is also true that Deep River work has an inevitable effect on the next generation of children and beyond. For me, the impact on our children—that is, on our future—is at the heart of why this work is so important.

Many years ago, when I first recognized that I had lost my inner bearings among the to-do's of young motherhood, I was aware only of needing to find myself, to make some time for stillness and the relief and reconnection I hoped it would bring. I wasn't thinking about whether this would be good or not good for my kids. All I knew was that although I loved caring for them, doing so was exhausting and draining me, and I needed to find my way back to the Deep River.

Now, in hindsight, I see that my insistent efforts back then to slow down and carve out time to go inward were not important just for me. They made me a better parent and they modeled something invaluable for my children. I often ask parents, and I know that parents often ask themselves, "Do you ever wonder what your hurried schedule is modeling for your children?"

I'm reminded of a *New Yorker* cartoon by Jack Ziegler of a man rushing out the front door of his house. As he pulls his son after him by the hand, the boy's feet are flying up in the air, his teddy bear has fallen out of his hand, his hat is about to drop to the ground, and his eyes are popping. In the caption, the dad is saying, "O.K., kid. Busy man here. Quality time. Here we go."[2] Another cartoon by Robert Weber shows a droopy-eyed mom sitting at the bedside of a droopy-eyed girl. She says to her daughter, "It's just exhaustion, sweetie. Everybody's got it."[3]

These cartoons are funny because they caricature issues familiar to so many of us. But for me, just under the laugh is a poignant sense of sorrow. What if we pause long enough to let ourselves see and feel what our information-saturated, 24/7, fast-track culture is doing to our children? Children's brains are designed to imitate, and children today are picking up, with frightening agility, the habits of multitasking, staying on the surface of things, and moving at high velocities. They are also showing signs of burnout at disturbingly young ages.

I am not going to dwell here on the litany of problems that children are dealing with, from substance abuse, self-mutilation, and Internet addiction to obesity, depression, and anxiety, to name just a few. I certainly don't place the cause of these many issues in young people's lives in any one factor, personal or societal. A complex web of interconnected influences gives rise to the challenges that the next generation faces. Nevertheless, I do believe that our culture's devotion to speed is a negative influence that exacerbates the others. We know for ourselves the price we pay in stress-related symptoms when we get caught up in the disease of a-thousand-things-to-do. Likewise, if we allow ourselves to look, we can see the signs of stress in our children when they are going too fast and doing too much. When we choose to slow down and simplify, it is usually with the intention of living a less stressful life. But there is more to it than that. For ourselves as well as for our children, the search for a slower pace of life comes not just from a need to experience *less* stress but also from a need to experience *more* depth and meaning. As a culture, we need to be asking not just "*How* do we slow down?" but "*Why?*"

What's at Stake:
Thinking, Feeling, and Listening Deeply

We don't slow down for its own sake; we slow down for the sake of what is gained when we do and what may be lost if we don't. At our current pace, we risk a future in which our ability to think deeply, feel deeply, and listen deeply—to one another and to ourselves— are seriously compromised. Thinking deeply requires undivided attention and time to focus on an idea, to mull it over and allow it to incubate as part of its development, to consider problems from many angles, to let understanding and wisdom ripen. This kind of attention and time is currently at risk, even at our universities, which are considered to be society's bastions of deep thinking.[4]

Feeling deeply also requires a slower pace; no time to feel our feelings is a hallmark of life lived at the surface. If the press of time short-circuits our ability to rejoice, express love, and feel gratitude, as well as to feel sorrow and grieve, we go numb. Our hearts shut down, and we lose not only our capacity for compassion but also our heart's ability to guide us to what matters most and the energy our feelings give us to act on what we care about. By allowing ourselves to feel and express our pain for others and for the world, we gain access to the wisdom, courage, and power that are needed for creative, effective responses to the problems that face us today.[5] As we saw in Chapter Six, with an open heart and Deep River access, we can transmute pain into compassionate power. But when we speed along the surface of life, we lose touch with the deep-down, ever-replenishing stream that feeds the taproot of both our caring and our power.

The ability to listen deeply to others is important for everything from success in personal relationships to world peace. Sometimes it seems as though the last thing we have time for is listening to one another. But when we take the time to listen with presence, not only do we foster harmony in our relationships, but we also invite those we listen to to contact their own depth. We become catalysts, helping them to access the Deep River. This is a gift we can give through listening deeply when we make time for and give our attention to another.

The Deep River process both requires and develops the ability to listen deeply to ourselves. Given the pace at which we are all moving, pausing to listen to our own inner promptings and to act on what we hear is becoming a rare and radical act. The wisdom we hear when we slow down and listen inwardly may not always make logical sense or draw approval from others. It takes courage, skill, and equanimity to attend to inner promptings when we are busy and when outer action is expected of us. But if we don't make time for inner listening, we risk being unable to draw from our best sources of creativity, intuition, and insight to solve problems in our lives and in our world.

I would like to be able to say with confidence that the next generation is growing up with the social conditions and personal skills they need in order to think, feel, and listen deeply. Right now, I can't say that this is true. Guiding children to develop these skills and creating conditions in our culture that foster them are essential challenges we face. Apple Computer's CEO Steve Jobs, in his commencement address at Stanford University in June 2005, had these words for the graduates: "Your time is limited. . . . Don't waste it living someone else's life. . . . Don't let the noise of others' opinions drown out your own inner voice. And most important, have the courage to follow your heart and intuition. They somehow already know what you truly want to become. Everything else is secondary."[6]

I loved reading this advice to look inward, especially because it came from one of the gurus of the information age. But it is not enough to inspire our young people with this kind of wisdom; we must ensure that our children and their children know what their inner voice is and how to find it. We need to create cultural conditions that make room to hear one's heart and intuition, so that they can be followed. We need to question and counter the seemingly inexorable rise on the speedometer of daily life. We need to pause and practice presence, and we need to influence our schools, workplaces, communities, businesses, and governments to do the same. We need to nurture in ourselves and then model and pass on the tools for touching the Deep River and drawing on those restorative waters to heal ourselves, our children, and our world.

Making a Difference

It is a daunting proposition indeed to transform a culture out of balance and a world in crisis. Once we have the tools to slow down and find balance and depth individually, we naturally begin to ask, "Do my individual efforts to slow down and touch the Deep River have any effect on the priorities of our culture and the state of the world?" I can't say with absolute certainty what effect our individual acts have on our collective reality. But I *can* say with certainty that when I draw from the Deep River in my daily life, it helps me and the people around me. When one Deep River group member makes a shift away from uncontrolled busyness and toward embracing depth, her example encourages others to do the same. Our efforts to change our pace and priorities have an observable ripple effect. And as writer Malcolm Gladwell asserts, if enough individuals make a change, there comes a "tipping point" when the shift becomes collective.[7]

Of course, change on a systemwide level will take more than multiple individual changes. For many struggling wage earners in America today, saying "Slow down" within the context of an economy driven by growth, profit, overconsumption, and increasing global competition is like saying "Come fly away" to a caged bird. We need transformation in our institutions at the local, national, and international levels. When it comes to large-scale change, it is a both-and rather than an either-or proposition. We need *both* many individuals' making changes in their own lives *and* institutions' making shifts in the priorities that shape their policies and practices.

Not all of us are in a position to directly effect change on an institutional level, but through our individual choices, we *all* can contribute to the potential "tipping point," toward shifting the priorities in our culture and toward healing our world. It's easy to feel hopeless or paralyzed when faced with the enormous suffering that sometimes seems to show up in every direction we look. There is an understandable temptation simply *not* to look—to turn away, to "get busy" with whatever task or distraction is at hand, or to keep ourselves buried in our own lives in a head-in-the-sand kind of way. In these moments when we want to shut down and pull back from the world, our ability to draw from the Deep River can help us to feel and to act on what we see rather than stay paralyzed or in denial. This is precisely where the connection lies between the many problems of our world and the resources of the Deep River realm. When we know how to slow down and go inward, we are able, first of all, to recognize and accept the natural feelings of hopelessness and overwhelm that can close our hearts. By befriending these feelings, we are in a better position both to allow our caring and to find a more empowered way to act on behalf of what matters to us. When we do take action, the Deep River realm offers the clarity, compassion, strength, and sense of purpose that allow us to respond to the needs of the world in our own meaningful way.

Our Unique Calling

It is a seeming paradox that the more we go inward and touch the Deep River, the more we are called to take the resources we find there out into the world. Jean, a science teacher and mother of two, came to a Deep River group at a time when she was feeling overwhelmed and out of balance due to stresses at work and at home. Her primary goal in the group was to create some time-in each day, to sit quietly and perhaps meditate. Very gradually, with many starts and stops, she finally began to have a regular quiet time each morning. Jean's time-in helped reduce her daily stress level, but it also had an unexpected effect. She explains: "I used to launch myself out of bed like a rubber band so I could have the *whole* day to get stuff done.

I never stopped long enough to say 'thank you' for having this day, at the start of each day. Now, when I look out at the trees as I sit still in the morning, I feel thankful—for my health, my family, a job, plenty to eat . . . and that sense of gratitude makes me want to *look* for ways to give back." With her newfound gratitude, Jean began to volunteer at the local food pantry. For her, this is a way to give back that arises directly out of her gratitude and addresses an issue she cares about deeply.

Over time, the wisdom of the Deep River dimension can gently guide us to find the part that is ours to play in healing the world. In my view, we all have a unique contribution to make. It might be caring for our children or for other family members, friends, or neighbors. It might be tending the piece of earth we inhabit, giving to our communities, or working directly to alleviate suffering. It might be creating or supporting art, organizations, or ideas that inspire others to think, feel, and listen deeply. We come to a sense of knowing about what our unique contribution is at any point in time by turning inward, getting quiet, and listening to the "still, small voice" within. This helps us answer the question "What is mine to do in this world?" We can hear what our particular call or way of responding to the needs before us might be rather than how we think we *should* respond or how a neighbor or friend or coworker responds. As one Deep River group member put it, "When I get quiet inside, I feel my connection to other people, and I'm reminded that it's just an illusion that we're not connected. When I'm tapped into that, it feels important to do my part and for everybody to do their part, because we *are* in this together. I don't have to change the world myself; I have to do what I can do. And that's what everybody can do."

Anchored in the Deep River

When we choose to respond to an inner call and begin to act and interact in the world, things don't always go smoothly. How do we find a sense of balance and equanimity, so as not to be defeated by the setbacks or overwhelmed by the difficulties that inevitably come with acting on what we care about? How do we find the courage and strength to stand up and speak out for what is important to us—or to hold quietly and persistently to what matters to us—in the face of discouragement, obstacles, opposition? Here, the cycle of "dropping down and returning" is invaluable. We drop down to the Deep River realm to reconnect with our sense of purpose and to tap a source of vitality and power that is greater than our individual strength. We can then return to what is ours to do with renewed energy and commitment, more perspective, and perhaps some creative solutions to the difficulties we have encountered.

Alex is a professor who enrolled in a Deep River group to help her through a job transition from one university to another. In addition to her teaching, Alex took on a new role as part of "what is hers to do." She is an expert on the history, culture, and politics of the Middle East, and she was asked to be a consultant to the U.S. military. This job raised many fears and presented many challenges; she says the Deep River work has given her tools both to deal with her fears and to rise to the challenges. When she works with the military, "dropping down and returning" is a lifeline:

> I'm in this overwhelming environment with hundreds of people in uniform, almost all men, most of them thinking of their adversary, looking to me for my perspective. I feel the weight of my responsibility, and it's an enormous strain on me. I wouldn't be able to do it without the inner work. Sometimes I step out of the room and stand in a corner someplace. (Fortunately there are so few women that usually a bathroom is a safe bet!) Even if I don't have very long, I take some time to be alone and quiet down, because I know how important it is. It taps me into a flow of deep, ancient wisdom and truth from human souls over thousands of years. When I think to myself, "What difference could I possibly make?" my mini time-in replenishes my hope and the strength to try to do the right thing. Even though I'm one small person—nobody, really—it restores my sense of connection to other people and my determination to do my part.

Alex's ability to anchor herself in "ancient long-standing truths" by tapping into the Deep River supports her in doing the challenging work she has been called to. And in her view, it contributes to the impact she is able to have. She says,

> When I pause before participating in these discussions, I envision actual people on the "other side"; I think about the countryside where I've been. And I also think about American soldiers who would be in some hunkered-down position if there were a war. I try to imagine what things are like from each point of view and concentrate on having compassion for each position. It's not an analytical exercise; it's engaging my heart. That's neither what my academic training nor what this military setting tells me to do. That comes from learning the value of orienting myself inwardly in order to be effective outwardly. Then, I speak with more authenticity to the officers, and I think that's part of why they listen to me.
>
> I'm certainly not just telling them what they want to hear; I would regard that as a really bad outcome. But I've been able to find common ground, to have compassion for them and respect for their point of view, often while telling them things they don't want to hear. The fact that they continue to listen to me and to ask me back at higher levels is because I have found a way to talk to them. And I know I've done that through my internal work.

Our Role as Women

It is particularly important that we women learn to draw on our inner resources of wisdom and compassion because women have a critical role to play in making the world a better place for ourselves and for future generations. The first way that this is true is straightforward: while both women's and men's roles are shifting, women are still by and large the primary guides and caretakers of the next generation—at home, at school, in day care. As such, what we model in these roles matters. We are well positioned as nurturers and teachers to guide our children toward thinking, feeling, and listening more deeply.

When women in my groups begin to work with the Deep River process, they often become more aware of the importance of their role in their family and beyond. One group member put it like this: "If I'm off, it seems like the mood of the whole family can go off." Likewise, when we are able to make room for Deep River nourishment and find our own balance, this in turn nourishes those around us. Anne Morrow Lindbergh understood well the ripple effect of finding her balance through taking time-in: "I must try to be alone for part of each year . . . and for part of each day . . . in order to keep my core, my center. . . . Woman must be still as the axis of a wheel in the midst of her activities. . . . She must be the pioneer in achieving this stillness, not only for her own salvation, but for the salvation of family life, of society, perhaps even of our civilization."[8]

The other way in which women have an essential role to play in effecting change has less to do with women as biological mothers or as humans in female bodies than it does with women as the dominant carriers of what might be called "feminine qualities"—traits and abilities such as empathy, relationship tending, collaboration, compassion, vulnerability, and intuition. Both women and men might have and express these traits, just as both might have and express what are referred to as "masculine qualities," such as individualism, assertiveness, decisiveness, competition, control, and rational-mind dominance. Our culture has placed high value on the masculine qualities and much less value on the feminine ones. It has been suggested that many of the challenges we face, including social injustice, environmental degradation, and the problems of globalization reflect an imbalance between masculine and feminine qualities. More balance could help restore health to our social and environmental systems. As women, we need the energy, strength, and sense of purpose that come from the Deep River to make sure these feminine qualities are added to the balance where they are needed. Alex's practice of slowing down and taking time-in while consulting to the army is a good example of drawing power from the Deep River and using it in the service of compassionate action.

Women, as well as men who are open to and have developed the feminine qualities, are a key force in the healing of our world. That fierce, protective "mother bear" love[9] is very powerful, and it is *that* kind of power—rising out of love for what is both vulnerable and precious—that we need in order to bring about a safer, more just, and peaceful world.

The Deep River: Flowing Forward

When I slow down and become still inside, I often touch a feeling of grief about the suffering all over the planet. At the same time, the renewing waters of the Deep River nourish in me the hope that, as difficult as the challenges are, we *can* save ourselves and heal the world. We *can* create and support the social conditions that enable future generations to think, feel, and listen deeply. It *is* possible to create a legacy of peace and reverence for life to leave for those who follow us. Knowing how to turn inward and draw on the deepest wisdom and compassion we can find is part of creating that legacy. To do so, we must break the cultural habit of sacrificing our inner lives for our outer lives, of giving up depth in deference to speed.

Of course, for this healing to occur, we need not only the inner resources of the Deep River but also the support of one another. When we take on what is ours to do and the going gets tough, sometimes it makes all the difference to be listened to and cheered on by someone else who understands and values what we're doing. Any gathering of two or more that cultivates presence, deep listening, and mutual respect can offer the kind of support we need to be forces for good in the world. We can give support one on one over tea or while taking a walk; we can give encouragement in mother's groups, healing circles, and community, school, and religious groups. We can give support on the job and in our communities. We can help one another to find moments of quiet renewal in our hurried world. The support we give one another for our inner work then paves the way for us to come together and act collectively to protect, nurture, and celebrate what we care about.

My hope for our children's children is that they will have more support from their culture and from one another for slowing down, attending inwardly, and living in ways that help sustain life on earth. The work each of us does to slow our pace and draw from the Deep River is part of creating that life-sustaining future. By attending to our deepest selves day to day, we not only receive nourishment but also plant the seeds of a much-needed alternative to prevailing cultural norms. May our inner work be a blessing, and may it help to bring about a more life-giving, just, and peaceful world for ourselves and one another, for our children, for our planet, for our future.

Victory Log

These pages are for you to use to begin recording your victories, as discussed in Chapter Three. A reminder: a victory is any shift, no matter how small, that you make toward a goal you've set for yourself. Recording your victories by writing them down is a helpful way to fix them in your awareness as positive reference points. When you're feeling discouraged or overwhelmed, it's helpful to have concrete evidence of positive choices you've already made. You don't need to make full-blown journal entries here unless you want to. Short notations will do; for example,

- I read the first three chapters of <u>Finding the Deep River Within</u> this aft.
- Took three deep breaths after coming home and before putting the groceries away.
- Tried the exercise of driving 5 mph more slowly than usual . . . and liked it! It calmed me down.

These pages are for you. May your victories be a source of strength and encouragement!

Any act of courage adds
courage to the universe.
—*Hermann Keyserling*

You gain strength, courage, and confidence
by every experience in which you really
stop to look fear in the face.
—*Eleanor Roosevelt*

It is not because things are difficult
that we do not dare; it is because we
do not dare that they are difficult.
—*Seneca*

By replacing "No way!" with "Maybe," we
open the door to mystery and to magic.
—*Julia Cameron*

The key to realizing a dream is to focus not on success but significance—and then even the small steps and little victories along your path will take on greater meaning.

—Oprah Winfrey

Each limit exceeded, each boundary crossed,
verifies that most limits are self-imposed, that
your potential and possibilities are far greater
than you have imagined, and that you are
capable of far more than you thought.
—*Robert Kriegel*

Nothing is so full of victory as patience.
—*Chinese proverb*

There is no royal road to anything. One
thing at a time, all things in succession.
That which grows fast, withers as rapidly.
That which grows slowly, endures.
—*Josiah Gilbert Holland*

Notes

Chapter One

1. I first saw the phrase "the disease of a-thousand-things-to-do" in Rice, J., "Why Play?" *Sojourners Magazine*, Jan.–Feb. 1997, p. 27.
2. Heart disease is the leading killer of women in the United States, according to *Making the Grade on Women's Health: A National and State-by-State Report Card 2004* (National Women's Law Center, Washington, D.C., and Oregon Health and Science University, Portland, Ore., 2004), p. 224. Women are twice as likely as men to experience migraines, according to Lucas, J., Schiller, J., and Benson, V., *Summary Health Statistics for U.S. Adults: National Health Interview Survey, 2001* (Vital Health Statistics, Series 10, No. 218) (Hyattsville, Md.: National Center for Health Statistics, 2004), p. 5.
3. Women are twice as likely as men to be depressed, and experts estimate that one in five women will have a depressive episode at some point in her life, according to Lombardi, L. "Hooked on Happiness: More Women Are Being Prescribed Anti-Depressants: Are We and Our Doctors Addicted to the Quick Fix for Feeling Good?" *Shape*, May 2002 (available at http://www.looksmartice skating.com/p/articles/mi_m0846/is_9_21/ai_84599102).
4. *Substance Abuse and the American Woman* (New York: National Center on Addiction and Substance Abuse, Columbia University, June 1996).

5. The Columbia University study listed in note 4 reports these figures: 21.5 million women in the United States smoke, 4.5 million are alcoholics or alcohol abusers, 3.5 million misuse prescription drugs, and 3.1 million regularly use illicit drugs. Chronic drinking among women has been on the rise since 1999, with 4.5 percent of women studied considered to be chronic drinkers—less than men, but the gap is rapidly closing.

6. Brach, T., *Radical Acceptance* (New York: Bantam Books, 2003), p. 5.

7. Brach, *Radical Acceptance*, p. 6.

8. Brach, *Radical Acceptance*, p. 3.

9. Brach, *Radical Acceptance*, p. 4.

10. Wasserman, D., *Boston Globe*, Apr. 24, 1995 (editorial cartoon).

11. Yow, E., "Hurry Up and Relax," *Self*, July 1996, p. 38.

12. Remy, M., Gutfeld, G., and Kita, J., "Simplify Your Life," *Prevention*, Sept. 1997, pp. 73–79.

13. Ventura, M., "The Age of Interruption," *Family Therapy Networker*, Jan.–Feb. 1995, p. 23.

14. Hallowell, E., "Overloaded Circuits: Why Smart People Underperform," *Harvard Business Review*, Jan. 2005, pp. 55–56.

15. Christakis, D., "Early Television Exposure and Subsequent Attentional Problems in Children," *Pediatrics*, Apr. 2004, *113*(4), 708–713.

16. Barron, J., "The First Angry Man," (interview with Sven Birkerts) *Detroit Monthly*, Nov. 1994, p. 60.

Chapter Two

1. Estés, C. P., *Women Who Run with the Wolves* (New York: Ballantine Books, 1992), p. 298.

2. Sarton, M., *Journal of a Solitude* (New York: Norton, 1973), p. 145.

3. Kidd, S. M., *The Mermaid Chair* (New York: Viking, 2005), p. 309.

4. Estés, *Women Who Run with the Wolves*, p. 265.

5. Estés, *Women Who Run with the Wolves*, p. 269.
6. Estés, *Women Who Run with the Wolves*, p. 277.
7. Sarton, *Journal of a Solitude*, p. 89.

Chapter Three

1. Rechtshaffen, S., *Time Shifting* (New York: Doubleday, 1996), pp. 21–32.
2. Rechtshaffen, *Time Shifting*, p. 26.
3. Cameron, J., *The Artist's Way: A Spiritual Path to Higher Creativity* (New York: Jeremy P. Tarcher/Perigee Books, 1992), pp. 9–18.
4. I first heard of the Victory Log in a talk by author and business consultant Bob Kriegel. He mentions it in all of his books. For more information, see www.kriegel.com.
5. James, W., and James, H. (contributors), *The Letters of William James*, Vol. 1 (Boston: Atlantic Monthly Press, 1920), p. 47.
6. I first heard the term *blocking belief* as part of a training session in EMDR (eye movement desensitization and reprocessing), a psychotherapy technique developed by Francine Shapiro. For more information, see www.emdria.org.

Chapter Four

1. Lindbergh, A. M., *Gift from the Sea* (New York: Vintage Books, 1955), p. 50.
2. L'Engle, M., *A Circle of Quiet* (New York: Farrar, Straus & Giroux, 1972), p. 4.
3. Lindbergh, *Gift from the Sea*, pp. 49–50.
4. Sarton, M., *After the Stroke: A Journal* (New York: Norton, 1988), p. 18.
5. Palmer, P., *The Courage to Teach* (San Francisco: Jossey-Bass, 1998), p. 65.
6. Sarton, M., *Journal of a Solitude* (New York: Norton, 1973), p. 81.

7. Bynner, W., *The Way of Life According to Lao Tzu* (New York: Capricorn Books, 1944), p. 55.

Chapter Five

1. Lindbergh, A. M., *Gift from the Sea* (New York: Vintage Books, 1955), pp. 55–56.
2. Mankoff, R., *New Yorker*, May 3, 1993.
3. Lindbergh, *Gift from the Sea*, p. 52.
4. Covey, S. R., *The 7 Habits of Highly Effective People* (New York: Simon & Schuster, 1989), p. 151.
5. Estés, C. P., *Women Who Run with the Wolves* (New York: Ballantine Books, 1992), p. 287.
6. The term *subpersonality* comes from the system of psychology called psychosynthesis. Psychosynthesis, developed in the early twentieth century by Italian psychiatrist Roberto Assagioli, is an integrative psychological framework that, among other things, works with inner parts or subpersonalities within a context of wholeness. The psychosynthesis model of the psyche includes both personal and transpersonal or spiritual aspects of the person and seeks to foster personal growth and self-awareness as part of the path toward psychological healing and spiritual awakening. For more information on psychosynthesis, see the Selected Reading, or visit the following Web sites:

www.synthesiscenter.org
www.psychosynthesisispaloalto.com
www.aap-psychosynthesis.org
www.psychosynthesis.org

Chapter Six

1. Jenna's "frozen" state is an example of dissociation, a mental process of separating from one's body or from particular feelings, thoughts, or urges. Dissociation exists on a continuum from the

natural dissociative moments we all have (such as missing an exit while driving because our attention is elsewhere) to the more extreme dissociation that is used as a means of coping with childhood trauma or abuse and that can continue into adulthood. If you think or know that you are prone to dissociation as a result of trauma or abuse, it is recommended that you seek the help of a mental health professional to assist you in moving toward difficult feelings. To find a trained therapist in your area, visit the Web site of the International Society for the Study of Dissociation: www.issd.org. For more information on dissociation and how to work with it, in layperson's terms, see Napier, N. J., *Getting Through the Day: Strategies for Adults Hurt as Children* (New York: Norton, 1993).

2. Chödrön, P., *The Places That Scare You: A Guide to Fearlessness in Difficult Times* (Boston: Shambhala, 2001), p. 23.

3. If you decide to seek professional help and have never done so, you might begin by asking for a referral from someone in your community whose judgment you trust—perhaps a primary care doctor, school counselor, minister, rabbi, priest, or friend who might know someone. There are also many online referral sources; in addition to the ISSD Web site in note 1, you might try www.emdria.org, www.apa.org, or www.networktherapy.org.

4. Greenspan, M., *Healing Through the Dark Emotions* (Boston: Shambhala, 2003), p. xii.

5. Chödrön, P., *When Things Fall Apart* (Boston: Shambhala, 1997), pp. 69–70.

6. Greenspan, *Healing Through the Dark Emotions*, p. 12.

7. Greenspan, *Healing Through the Dark Emotions*, p. 46.

Chapter Seven

1. Guisewite, C., "Cathy," *San Jose Mercury*, Aug. 1993.

2. Lamott, A., *Bird by Bird* (New York: Anchor Books, 1995), pp. 28–29.

3. Woodman, M., *Addiction to Perfection: The Still Unravished Bride* (Toronto: Inner City Books, 1982), p. 53.

4. Lamott, A., *Plan B: Further Thoughts on Faith* (New York: Riverhead Books, 2005), p. 68.

5. Cameron, J., *The Artist's Way: A Spiritual Path to Higher Creativity* (New York: Jeremy P. Tarcher/Perigee Books, 1992), pp. 11–12.

6. Estés, C. P., *Women Who Run with the Wolves* (New York: Ballantine Books, 1992), pp. 306–307.

7. Woodman, *Addiction to Perfection*, p. 7.

8. Chödrön, P., *The Wisdom of No Escape and the Path of Loving-Kindness* (Boston: Shambhala, 1991), pp. 6–7.

9. Salzberg, S., *Lovingkindness: The Revolutionary Art of Happiness* (Boston: Shambhala, 1995), pp. 42–43.

10. Rogers, C., *On Becoming a Person* (New York: Houghton Mifflin, 1961), p. 17.

11. Chödrön, P., *The Places That Scare You* (Boston, Shambhala, 2001), pp. 24–25.

12. Paraphrased from Chödrön, P., *When Things Fall Apart: Heart Advice for Difficult Times* (Boston: Shambala, 1997), p. 17.

13. Kinnell, G., *Mortal Acts, Mortal Words* (Boston: Houghton Mifflin, 1980), p. 9.

14. Thanks to Will Zangwill for the idea of listening to a disturbing inner voice as if listening to "Donald Duck on helium."

15. Thanks to Rick Carlson and Wayne Dyer for the saying "Don't sweat the small stuff—and it's all small stuff." See Carlson, R., *Don't Sweat the Small Stuff—and It's All Small Stuff* (New York: Hyperion, 1997). [In his book, Carlson credits Dyer with the phrase.]

16. Thanks to Jay Livingston and Ray Evans for the title phrase from their song *Que Sera Sera.*

17. Thanks to Tara Brach for the sentence "Nothing is wrong," from her book *Radical Acceptance* (New York: Bantam Books, 2003), p. 75.

18. Lawrence, R. G., "Wabi-Sabi: The Art of Imperfection," *Natural Home*, May–June 2001, paragraph 1; quoted in *Utne Magazine*, Sept.–Oct. 2001, p. 48.
19. Lawrence, R. G., "Wabi-Sabi," paragraph 4; quoted in *Utne Magazine*, Sept.–Oct. 2001, p. 48.

Chapter Eight

1. Kabat-Zinn, J., *Wherever You Go, There You Are: Mindfulness Meditation in Everyday Life* (New York: Hyperion, 1994), p. 176.
2. Dobisz, J., *The Wisdom of Solitude* (San Francisco: HarperSanFrancisco, 2004), pp. 120–121.
3. Kabat-Zinn, J., *Coming to Our Senses* (New York: Hyperion, 2005), p. 82.
4. Nhat Hanh, T., and Vo-Dinh, M. *The Miracle of Mindfulness* (Boston: Beacon Press, 1975), pp. 4–5.
5. Shellenbarger, S., "Juggling Too Many Tasks Could Make You Stupid" (www.CareerJournal.com), 2/28/2003.
6. Miller, H., *Rosy Crucifixion*, Book 2: *Plexus* (reprint ed.) (New York: Grove Press, 1987), p. 53.
7. Bhikkhu, A. *Silent Rain* (Redwood Valley, Calif.: Abhayagiri Buddhist Monastery, 1996), p. 31.
8. Proust, M. *Remembrance of Things Past*, trans. by Moncrieff, C.K.S. and Kilmartin, T. (New York: Vintage Books, 1982) Vol. 3, p. 260.
9. Dobisz, *The Wisdom of Solitude*, pp. 120–121.
10. M. McDonald, talk given at Insight Meditation Society, Barre, Mass., June 2004.
11. Oliver, M., *Blue Pastures* (New York: Harcourt, Brace, 1995), pp. 1–2.
12. In the Selected Reading section "On Practicing Presence, Concentration, and Meditation," see especially the works by Joseph Goldstein, Larry Rosenberg, Jon Kabat-Zinn, or Roger Walsh for instruction on developing concentration.

13. Thoreau, H., *Walden* (New York: Houghton Mifflin, 1995), p. 324.
14. Wilson, G., *New Yorker*, Aug. 25, 1980.
15. Walsh, R., *Essential Spirituality: The 7 Central Practices to Awaken Heart and Mind* (New York: Wiley, 1999), p. 159.
16. I first saw this exercise in Roger Walsh's *Essential Spirituality*, p. 156.
17. Hass, R., *The Essential Haiku: Versions of Basho, Buson, and Issa* (New York: Ecco, 1994), p. 11.

Chapter Nine

1. Rice, J., "Why Play?" *Sojourners Magazine*, Jan.–Feb. 1997, p. 25.
2. Canellos, P. S., "Many Longing for Clintonesque Leisure," *Boston Globe*, Aug. 18, 1997, pp. A1, A8.
3. Galinsky, E., Bond, J., Kim, S., Backon, L., Browfield, E., and Sakai, K., *Overwork in America: When the Way We Work Becomes Too Much* (New York: Families and Work Institute, 2004). The executive summary of this report is available at www.familiesand work.org. This study also showed that 28 percent of the female employees in the study received no paid vacation, a fact that would compound women's difficulty in finding time for play.
4. Peterson, B., *Nature and Other Mothers* (New York: Ballantine Books, 1995), p. 163.
5. Peterson, *Nature and Other Mothers*, p. 166.
6. Peterson, *Nature and Other Mothers*, p. 167.
7. Cameron, J., *The Artist's Way: A Spiritual Path to Higher Creativity* (New York: Jeremy P. Tarcher/Perigee Books, 1992), pp. 100–102.

Chapter Ten

1. Merton, T., *The Sign of Jonas* (New York: Harcourt, 2002), p. 256.
2. Ziegler, J., *New Yorker*, Nov. 4, 2002.

3. Weber, R., *New Yorker*, Mar. 27, 1995.

4. The vast majority in a survey of 100 professors at six universities no longer read as broadly or as deeply and reflectively as they used to or as they'd like to. Asked about the possible effect on their students, they made comments such as these: "My students have lost the capacity to take voice and articulate themselves in their writing. . . . There's just no depth to their reading, often, and no depth to their sense of 'What do I do with all this material? How do I focus?'" See Menzies, H., "Dumbed Down on Campus Bit by Bit: Are PCs Making Professors More Absent-Minded?" *Toronto Star*, May 1, 2005, p. D-1.

    For more information, see Heather Menzies's book *No Time: Stress and the Crisis of Modern Life* (Vancouver, Canada: Douglas & McIntyre, 2005).

5. For more on working with pain and despair about the state of the world, see Joanna Macy's book *Despair and Personal Power in the Nuclear Age* (Philadelphia: New Society, 1983), which describes her groundbreaking work on despair and empowerment.

6. Jobs, S., commencement address, Stanford University, June 12, 2005; excerpted in *Timeline*, Sept.–Oct. 2005, no. 83, p. 23.

7. Gladwell, M., *The Tipping Point: How Little Things Can Make a Big Difference* (New York: Little, Brown, 2000).

8. Lindbergh, A. M. *Gift from the Sea* (New York: Vintage Books, 1955), pp. 58–59.

9. I don't know where the reference to "mother bear" originated. It has been used by Elizabeth Sawen of the Sustainability Institute (www.sustainabilityinstitute.org), Christiane Northrup (www.dr northrup.com), Jean Shinoda Bolen (www.jeanbolen.com), and Women's Well cofounder and psychotherapist Anne Yeomans (www.womenswell.org) as a way to describe women's fierce instinct to protect children and other vulnerable beings when they are in danger and as a call to women to make a bold and unwavering commitment to rebalancing the masculine and feminine qualities on earth.

Selected Reading

On the Power of 24/7 Culture

Burns, Leland Smith. *Busy Bodies: Why Our Time-Obsessed Society Keeps Us Running in Place*. New York: Norton, 1993.

Gleick, James. *Faster: The Acceleration of Just About Everything*. New York: Vintage, 2000.

Honoré, Carl. *In Praise of Slowness: How a Worldwide Movement Is Challenging the Cult of Speed*. San Francisco: HarperSanFrancisco, 2004.

Lara, Adair. *Slowing Down in a Speeded-Up World*. Berkeley, Calif.: Conari Press, 1994.

Menzies, Heather. *No Time: Stress and the Crisis of Modern Life*. Vancouver, Canada: Douglas & McIntyre, 2005.

On Slowing Down and Achieving Balance in Everyday Life

Bender, Sue. *Everyday Sacred: A Woman's Journey Home*. San Francisco: HarperSanFrancisco, 1995.

Eyre, Richard M., and Linda Eyre. *Lifebalance: Priority Balance, Attitude Balance, Goal Balance in All Areas of Your Life*. New York: Ballantine Books, 1988.

Grudin, Robert. *Time and the Art of Living*. New York: Ticknor & Fields, 1988.

Moore, Thomas. *The Re-Enchantment of Everyday Life*. New York: HarperCollins, 1996.

Rechtschaffen, Stephan. *Time Shifting: Creating More Time to Enjoy Your Life*. New York: Doubleday, 1996.

St. James, Elaine. *Inner Simplicity: 100 Ways to Regain Peace and Nourish Your Soul*. New York: Hyperion, 1995.

St. James, Elaine. *Living the Simple Life: A Guide to Scaling Down and Enjoying More*. New York: Hyperion, 1996.

Swenson, Richard A. *Margin: Restoring Emotional, Physical, Financial and Time Reserves*. Colorado Springs, Colo.: NavPress, 2004.

On Keeping a Journal

Baldwin, Christina. *Life's Companion: Journal Writing as a Spiritual Quest.* New York: Bantam Books, 1991.

Baldwin, Christina. *One to One: Self-Understanding Through Journal Writing.* New York: M. Evans, 1991.

Also read about the practice of writing "morning pages" in Julia Cameron's *The Artist's Way* and *The Vein of Gold,* listed under "On Creativity and Doing Something You Love."

On Taking Time-In

André, Rae. *Positive Solitude: A Practical Program for Mastering Loneliness and Achieving Self-Fulfillment.* New York: HarperCollins, 1991.

Cooper, David A. *Silence, Simplicity and Solitude: A Complete Guide to Spiritual Retreat.* Woodstock, Vt.: SkyLight Paths, 1999.

Dowrick, Stephanie. *Intimacy and Solitude: Balancing Closeness and Independence.* New York: Norton, 1991.

Louden, Jennifer. *The Woman's Retreat Book: A Guide to Restoring, Rediscovering, and Reawakening Your True Self—In a Moment, an Hour, a Day, or a Weekend.* San Francisco: HarperSanFrancisco, 2005.

Taylor, Barbara E. *Silence: Making the Journey to Inner Quiet.* Philadelphia: Innisfree Press, 1997.

Women's Accounts of Retreat or Taking Time-In

Anderson, Joan. *A Year by the Sea: Thoughts of an Unfinished Woman.* New York: Broadway Books, 2000.

Bender, Sue. *Plain and Simple: A Woman's Journey to the Amish.* San Francisco: HarperSanFrancisco, 1989.

Dobisz, Jan. *The Wisdom of Solitude: A Zen Retreat in the Woods.* San Francisco: HarperSanFrancisco, 2004.

Koller, Alice. *An Unknown Woman: A Journey to Self-Discovery.* New York: Holt, Rinehart & Winston, 1981.

Norris, Kathleen. *The Cloister Walk.* New York: Riverhead Books, 1996.

Sarton, May. *Journal of a Solitude.* New York: Norton, 1973.

On Befriending Feelings

Bennett-Goleman, Tara. *Emotional Alchemy: How the Mind Can Heal the Heart.* New York: Harmony Books, 2001.

Brach, Tara. *Radical Acceptance: Embracing Your Life with the Heart of a Buddha*. New York: Bantam Books, 2003.

Chödrön, Pema. *The Wisdom of No Escape and the Path of Loving-Kindness*. Boston: Shambhala, 1991.

Chödrön, Pema. *Start Where You Are: A Guide to Compassionate Living*. Boston: Shambhala, 1994.

Chödrön, Pema. *When Things Fall Apart: Heart Advice for Difficult Times*. Boston: Shambhala, 1997.

Chödrön, Pema. *The Places That Scare You: A Guide to Fearlessness in Difficult Times*. Boston: Shambhala, 2001.

Greenspan, Miriam. *Healing Through the Dark Emotions: The Wisdom of Grief, Fear, and Despair*. Boston: Shambhala, 2003.

Macy, Joanna. *Despair and Personal Power in the Nuclear Age*. Philadelphia: New Society, 1983.

Moore, Thomas. *Care of the Soul: A Guide for Cultivating Depth and Sacredness in Everyday Life*. New York: Walker, 1993.

Nelson, John E., and Andrea Nelson. *Sacred Sorrows: Embracing and Transforming Depression*. New York: Putnam, 1996.

On Taming Expectations

Brach, Tara. *Radical Acceptance: Embracing Your Life with the Heart of a Buddha*. New York: Bantam Books, 2003.

Chödrön, Pema. *The Wisdom of No Escape and the Path of Loving-Kindness*. Boston: Shambhala, 1991.

Chödrön, Pema. *Start Where You Are: A Guide to Compassionate Living*. Boston: Shambhala, 1994.

Chödrön, Pema. *The Places That Scare You: A Guide to Fearlessness in Difficult Times*. Boston: Shambhala, 2001.

Chödrön, Pema. *When Things Fall Apart: Heart Advice for Difficult Times*. Boston: Shambhala, 1997.

Kushner, Harold S. *How Good Do We Have to Be? A New Understanding of Guilt and Forgiveness*. Boston: Little, Brown, 1996.

Ladner, Lorne. *The Lost Art of Compassion*. San Francisco: HarperSanFrancisco, 2004.

Salzberg, Sharon. *Lovingkindness: The Revolutionary Art of Happiness*. Boston: Shambhala, 1995.

Woodman, Marion. *Addiction to Perfection: The Still Unravished Bride*. Toronto: Inner City Books, 1982.

On Practicing Presence, Concentration, and Meditation

Beck, Charlotte Joko, and Steve Smith. *Everyday Zen: Love and Work*. San Francisco: HarperSanFrancisco, 1989.

Boorstein, Sylvia. *It's Easier Than You Think: The Buddhist Way to Happiness*. San Francisco: HarperSanFrancisco, 1995.

Goldstein, Joseph. *Insight Meditation: The Practice of Freedom*. Boston: Shambhala, 2003.

Goldstein, Joseph, and Jack Kornfield. *The Path of Insight Meditation*. Boston: Shambhala, 1995.

Kabat-Zinn, Jon. *Coming to Our Senses: Healing Ourselves and the World Through Mindfulness*. New York: Hyperion, 2005.

Kabat-Zinn, Jon. *Wherever You Go, There You Are: Mindfulness Meditation in Everyday Life*. New York: Hyperion, 2005.

Kabat-Zinn, Jon. *Full Catastrophe Living: Using the Wisdom of Your Body and Mind to Face Stress, Pain, and Illness*. New York: Delta, 1990.

Levine, Stephen. *A Gradual Awakening*. New York: Anchor Books, 1989.

Nhat Hanh, Thich. *Present Moment, Wonderful Moment: Mindfulness Verses for Daily Living*. Berkeley, Calif.: Parallax, 1990.

Nhat Hanh, Thich. *Peace Is Every Step: The Path of Mindfulness in Everyday Life*. New York: Bantam Books, 1991.

Nhat Hanh, Thich, and Rachel Neumann. *Being Peace*. Berkeley, Calif.: Parallax, 2005.

Nhat Hanh, Thich, and Vo-Dinh Mai. *The Miracle of Mindfulness: A Manual on Meditation*. Boston: Beacon Press, 1975.

Rosenberg, Larry, and David Guy. *Breath by Breath: The Liberating Practice of Insight Meditation*. Boston: Shambhala, 1998.

Roy, Denise. *Momfulness: Mothering with Mindfulness, Compassion, and Grace*. San Francisco: Jossey-Bass, 2007.

Walsh, Roger. *Essential Spirituality: The 7 Central Practices to Awaken Heart and Mind*. New York: Wiley, 1999.

On Practicing Presence and Parenting

Doe, Mimi. *Busy but Balanced: Practical and Inspirational Ways to Create a Calmer, Closer Family*. New York: St. Martins Griffin, 2001.

Kabat-Zinn, Myla, and Jon Kabat-Zinn. *Everyday Blessings: The Inner Work of Mindful Parenting*. New York: Hyperion, 1997.

Napthali, Sarah. *Buddhism for Mothers: A Calm Approach to Caring for Yourself and Your Children*. Crows Nest, N.S.W., Australia: Allen & Unwin, 2003.

On Creativity and Doing Something You Love

Beck, Martha. *Finding Your Own North Star: Claiming the Life You Were Meant to Live*. New York: Crown, 2001.

Bennett, Hal Zina, and Susan J. Sparrow. *Follow Your Bliss*. New York: Avon Books, 1990.

Cameron, Julia. *The Artist's Way: A Spiritual Path to Higher Creativity*. New York: Jeremy P. Tarcher/Perigee Books, 1992.

Cameron, Julia. *The Vein of Gold: A Journey to Your Creative Heart*. New York: Putnam, 1996.

Sher, Barbara, and Barbara Smith. *I Could Do Anything If I Only Knew What It Was: How to Discover What You Really Want and How to Get It*. New York: Delacorte Press, 1994.

Wakefield, Dan. *Creating from the Spirit: Living Each Day as a Creative Act*. New York: Ballantine Books, 1996.

On Change in Our Culture and for Our Future

Bolen, Jean Shinoda. *Urgent Message from Mother: Gather the Women, Save the World*. York Beach, Maine: Conari Press, 2005.

Durning, Alan Thein. *How Much is Enough? The Consumer Society and the Future of the Earth*. New York: Norton, 1992.

Flinders, Carol L. *The Values of Belonging: Rediscovering Balance, Mutuality, Intuition, and Wholeness in a Competitive World*. San Francisco: HarperSanFrancisco, 2002.

Freed, Rachael. *Women's Lives, Women's Legacies: Passing Your Beliefs and Blessings to Future Generations: Creating Your Own Spiritual-Ethical Will*. Minneapolis, Minn.: Fairview Press, 2003.

Freed, Rachael. *The Women's Legacies Workbook for the Busy Woman: Breaking the Silence: Weaving Blessings and Words of Wisdom for Future Generations*. Minneapolis, Minn.: Minerva Press, 2005.

Macy, Joanna, and Molly Young Brown. *Coming Back to Life: Practices to Reconnect Our Lives, Our World*. Stony Creek, Conn.: New Society, 1998.

Wachtel, Paul L. *The Poverty of Affluence: A Psychological Portrait of the American Way of Life*. Philadelphia: New Society, 1989.

Primarily for Women

Christ, Carol P. *Diving Deep and Surfacing: Women Writers on Spiritual Quest*. Boston: Beacon Press, 1980.

Domar, Alice D., and Henry Dreher. *Healing Mind, Healthy Woman: Using the Mind-Body Connection to Manage Stress and Take Control of Your Life*. New York: Henry Holt, 1996.

Domar, Alice D., and Henry Dreher. *Self-Nurture: Learning to Care for Yourself as Effectively as You Care for Everyone Else*. New York: Viking Press, 2000.

Duerk, Judith. *Circle of Stones: Woman's Journey to Herself*. Makawao, Hawaii: Inner Ocean, 2004.

Duerk, Judith. *I Sit Listening to the Wind: Woman's Encounter Within Herself*. Makawao, Hawaii: Inner Ocean, 2005.

Estés, Clarissa Pinkola. *Women Who Run with the Wolves: Myths and Stories of the Wild Woman Archetype*. New York: Ballantine Books, 1992.

Firman, Julie, and Dorothy Firman. *Daughters and Mothers: Making It Work*. Deerfield Beach, Fla.: Health Communications, Inc., 2003.

Flinders, Carol. *At the Root of This Longing: Reconciling a Spiritual Hunger with a Feminist Thirst*. San Francisco: HarperSanFrancisco, 1998.

Hirsch, Kathleen. *A Sabbath Life: A Woman's Search for Wholeness*. New York: North Point Press, 2001.

Lindbergh, Anne Morrow. *Gift from the Sea*. New York: Vintage Books, 1955.

Louden, Jennifer. *Comfort Secrets for Busy Women: Finding Your Way When Your Life Is Overflowing*. Naperville, Ill.: Sourcebooks, 2003.

Van Steenhouse, Andrea, and Doris A. Fuller. *A Woman's Guide to a Simpler Life*. New York: Three Rivers Press, 1997.

Woodman, Marion, with Jill Melnick. *Coming Home to Myself: Reflections for Nurturing a Woman's Body and Soul*. Berkeley: Conari Press, 2001.

On Psychosynthesis

Assagioli, Roberto. *Psychosynthesis: A Manual of Principles and Techniques*. New York: Hobbs, Dorman, 1965.

Brown, Molly Young. *Growing Whole: Self-Realization on an Endangered Planet*. New York: HarperCollins, 1993.

Ferrucci, Piero. *What We May Be: Techniques for Psychological and Spiritual Growth*. Los Angeles: Jeremy P. Tarcher, 1982.

Firman, John, and Ann Gila. *Psychosynthesis: A Psychology of the Spirit*. Albany: State University of New York Press, 2002.

Gordon, Richard. *A Psychosynthesis Primer: The Path to the Self*. Self-published, Seattle, 1991.

Weiser, John, and Thomas Yeomans (eds.). *Psychosynthesis in the Helping Professions: Now and in the Future*.

Weiser, John, and Thomas Yeomans (eds.). *Readings in Psychosynthesis: Theory, Process and Practice*.

All of the titles in the Psychosynthesis category can be ordered at www.synthesis center.org. In Europe, visit www.psychosynthesis.org.

Other Selected Readings

Amaro Bhikkhu. *Silent Rain*. Redwood Valley, Calif.: Abhayagiri Buddhist Monastery, 1996.

Cousineau, Phil, and Eric Lawton. *The Soul Aflame: A Modern Book of Hours*. Berkeley, Calif.: Conari Press, 1999.

Covey, Stephen R. *The 7 Habits of Highly Effective People*. New York: Simon & Schuster, 1989.

Hilsinger, Serena S., and Lois Brynes (eds.). *The Selected Poems of May Sarton*. New York: Norton, 1978.

Kristan, Pamela. *The Spirit of Getting Organized: 12 Skills to Find Meaning and Power in Your Stuff*. Boston: Red Wheel, 2003.

Lamott, Anne. *Bird by Bird: Some Instructions on Writing and Life*. New York: Anchor Books, 1995.

Lamott, Anne. *Plan B: Further Thoughts on Faith*. New York: Riverhead Books, 2005.

Merton, Thomas. *Thoughts in Solitude*. New York: Farrar, Straus & Giroux, 1999.

Oliver, Mary. *New and Selected Poems*. Boston: Beacon Press, 1992.

Palmer, Parker J. *A Hidden Wholeness: The Journey Toward an Undivided Life*. San Francisco: Jossey-Bass, 2004.

Paul, Marilyn. *It's Hard to Make a Difference When You Can't Find Your Keys: The Seven-Step Path to Becoming Truly Organized*. New York: Viking Compass, 2003.

Remen, Rachel Naomi. *Kitchen Table Wisdom: Stories That Heal*. New York: Riverhead Books, 1996.

Remen, Rachel Naomi. *My Grandfather's Blessings: Stories of Strength, Refuge, and Belonging*. New York: Riverhead Books, 2000.

Richardson, Cheryl. *Take Time for Your Life: A Personal Coach's Seven-Step Program for Creating the Life You Want*. New York: Broadway Books, 1998.

Rumi, Jalal Al-Din. *The Illuminated Rumi*. (Coleman Barks, trans.; Michael Green, illus.). New York: Broadway Books, 1997.

Sarton, May. *Selected Poems of May Sarton*. New York: Norton, 1978.

Steindl-Rast, Brother David. *Gratefulness, the Heart of Prayer: An Approach to Life in Fullness*. New York: Paulist Press, 1984.

Thoreau, Henry D. *Walden; or, Life in the Woods*. New York: Houghton Mifflin, 1995.

Yeomans, Thomas. *On Earth Alive*. Concord, Mass.: Morning Star Press, 2000.

The Author

Abby Seixas has been a psychotherapist in private practice for over twenty-five years, working as a consultant and clinical psychotherapy supervisor at training centers in the United States and abroad, including England, the Netherlands, and Russia. For the last twelve years, her work has focused on helping women learn and practice the art of slowing down through public talks, retreats, workshops, and her popular Deep River™ groups. She has appeared on NBC's *The Today Show* and the Hallmark channel, and her work has been featured in national and local print media, including O. *The Oprah Magazine, Self, Body + Soul, Woman's Day* and *The Boston Globe.* She is the mother of two grown children and lives with her husband near Boston, Massachusetts.

Index

Want to Dive Deeper?

If this book inspires comments or questions, I welcome hearing from you. Please visit my Web site (www.deepriverwithin.com) to share your thoughts or a Deep River story of your own, or for more information about

- Speaking engagements for conferences; civic or religious organizations; or parents', women's, or other groups
- Deep River™ workshops or retreats
- Starting a Deep River peer group in your area
- Training for helping professionals in leading Deep River groups

Thank you!

—Abby Seixas